BEARS
to Cherish

Craftworld Books

Contents

Arctophilia

a Passion for Bears

Arctophilia, a passion for bears

There are people who set out to become arctophiles, individuals who actually decide consciously to become recognised as serious collectors of bears. For most of us though, it a more gradual submission.

The seed is planted in early childhood – you either had a bear or you didn't. If you did, you remember it fondly and indeed may still possess it. Either way you have the motive for beginning a collection. Your (now rather worn) companion of long standing may need a new friend or if he has long since disappeared, you may be attempting to replace him. And if you never had one, well what better reason for getting one now?

Frequently, the next is given to you by a well-intentioned friend. All of a sudden you become 'bear-aware'. They leap out at you from advertisements, greeting cards and calenders. You catch yourself looking in the local toy store. Then when a member of the family (usually a teenager) decides to abandon theirs, you adopt it – only until they have a child of their own. By this time the symptoms of arctophilia are becoming obvious to your nearest and dearest. Even if you are unwilling to admit it yourself, they happily latch onto the idea of a bear as an ideal gift. What can you do?

Succumb graciously. A bear is a wonderful present to receive – it is a permanent hug from the person who gave it to you, and a safe distraction for the next unruly child who may come to visit.

Arctophiles know that the sentimental value far outweighs the dollars spent. The cheapest mass-production toy is just as valid and individual as the most expensive Steiff. Herein lies the reason for the popularity of bears. Each has its own personality and the genuine collector will recognise a kindred spirit.

A particular look, maker or country of origin will appeal to one collector and may be of little interest to another. Just as each bear is individual, so is the taste of each collector. Some do not discriminate at all while others will attempt to be rigid specialists. Even self-limited collections of one genre can be vast – the variety produced by manufacturers over the past 90 years is being constantly expanded by today's artists. The related production of 'bearabilia' is now collectable in its own right.

Size and price become the most common boundaries for collectors. Within these boundaries an especially appealing bear can overcome such considerations as age, condition, pedigree and family disapproval. A normally sane and balanced person (if an arctophile at heart) can be completely captivated by a scruffy amputee that has been literally loved to bits by a previous owner. That same person can also appreciate the pristine (and therefore rare) antique teddy, long orphaned by an unfortunate child and never hugged. A quirky expression or inspired design can make you reach out to touch a bear, which is perhaps why they are so attractive in today's isolationist world.

So whether you know a closet collector (still in denial) or a flamboyant exhibitionist, be wary as arctophilia is highly contagious.

ANTIQUE BEARS

American, English and German brands are the most recognisable and the most popular. Bears carrying makers' marks are generally accorded more value and, if unmarked, may be attributed to a particular factory only by an expert.

There are many excellent reference books available now, the most valuable to the novice collector being a broad-range encyclopedia with plenty of pictures.

Also, the condition of any antique bear (pre-1940) should be reflected in the price.

EARLY MODERNS

The 1940s and '50s saw the rebuilding and enormous growth of the toy industry. World War II generated rapid developments in communications and transport as well as the technology to produce synthetic fabrics. In Britain, lightweight kapok, which had been used to insulate flying suits, was hijacked and used as stuffing for bears. Children of the Depression years became parents in the '50s and the children's toys are often extravagant examples of the booming post-war economies. Britain and Europe clung to the traditional mohairs, but America embraced the new synthetics in the '50s.

MODERNS

The 1960s saw major changes in the shapes and styles of bears. The influence of television spread rapidly. Children's cartoon characters, created for television or adapted from literature, became available to the mass market. In order to keep prices down, factories moved production east, firstly to Hong Kong, then Taiwan, Korea and now mainland China. The labour-intensive jointed bears gave way to softer unjointed toys. American design influences became more noticeable in the European bears. Mass-produced brands took a major share of the world market and the more expensive (mostly European) bears were taken more seriously by collectors. Steiff and Merrythought, Hermann and Canterbury and a host of others have established international reputations for the quality and collectability of their bears.

ARTIST BEARS

Over the past two decades a growing number of bear artists have been creating their own bears for sale. Production is usually very slow, mostly one of a kind or small, limited editions of five to 50. The most labour-intensive, hand-sewn bears are fairly rare these days. Most artists prefer to use a sewing machine for at least part of their work. Some use outworkers for jointing, sewing up or stuffing and the artists do the finishing, trimming and features by hand to achieve their individual look.

DESIGNER BEARS

Some factories produce bears designed by well-known artists. It is usual for the artist to create the pattern and supply a sample for the factory to copy. However, if the designer is not a bear maker, an original concept may be handed over to a pattern maker who merely uses the designer's name.

LIMITED EDITIONS

Whether it is produced by a manufacturer or an artist, the smaller the edition, the more collectable the bear.

BEARABILIA

Teddy bears in materials other than fur fabric, anything from carved wood to crystal or as a decoration for many everyday items, can form interesting collections. Porcelain and postcards, teaspoons and toiletries all offer a wide range of teddy nostalgia. ❖

GENERAL STORE

Warm and
Cuddly

Reuben

Reuben, by British bear artist Jo Green, is designed to work well dressed, or 'au naturel'. He is made from English sparse mohair but the pattern works equally well with straight or distressed fur.

PREPARATION

❖

Read all the information carefully before you begin. Trace the pattern from the pattern sheet onto cardboard to make templates, transferring all markings. Mark the direction of the pile on the back of the fabric and match the arrows on the pattern to the direction of the pile. Trace around pieces and cut out carefully, cutting only the backing fabric. A 5mm seam allowance is included in the pattern. Trim the fur from the seam allowances before stitching.

HEAD

❖

Pin and sew side head pieces together from the top of the nose down the centre front seam, to the base of the neck. Pin the gusset in position, matching the centre-front mark to the seam, and lining the neck edges. Stitch from the centre front to the back on both sides, easing to fit, being careful not to stretch the fabric, If you're not a very experienced sewer, it is advisable to tack the gusset in place before you stitch, since accuracy is crucial to achieve a well-shaped head. Turn the head right side out and stuff firmly, starting with the nose and muzzle. Using double extra-strong thread, sew a running stitch around the neck, 5mm from the edge. Attach a washer and side to one of the cotter pins and insert into the head, then draw up the gathering thread tightly around the shank of the cotter pin, and secure with slipknots.

BODY

❖

Sew darts, then pin and sew the body pieces together, leaving the openings at the neck edge and the back as indicated on the pattern. Using an awl or knitting needle, make joint holes, then turn right side out.

LIMBS

❖

Pin and sew paw pads to the inner arms, then join inner and outer arms, leaving an opening as indicated, for stuffing. Sew leg pieces together, again, leaving an opening for stuffing, then attach foot pads, easing to fit. Make joint holes as before.

EARS

❖

Select preferred ear size, the larger having been used for our bear. Pin and Stitched the curved edge, clip corners and turn right side out. Oversew the raw edges together across the base.

EMBROIDERING THE NOSE

❖

Cut away the fur from the nose and muzzle, cutting just a little at a time and making sure the trimming is symmetrical. Now work the nose and mouth using the Perlé thread. Use a close, even satin stitch for the nose. You can also use the same thread to form the mouth with straight stitches.

FINISHED SIZE

• 25.5cm (10in)

MATERIALS

• 15cm x 67.5cm (6in x 26½in) fur fabric
• 11.5cm x 7.5cm (4½in x 3in) fabric for paws such as ultrasuede, felt or velvet
• Matching sewing threads,
• 5x20mm (¾in) wooden joints with cotter pins
• Long-nose pliers
• 8mm eyes
• Extra strong thread
• Perlé thread in matching colour for nose and mouth
• Polyester stuffing
• Stuffing tool
• Awl or knitting needle
• General sewing requirements

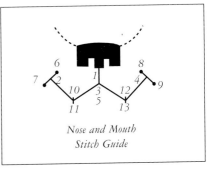

Nose and Mouth Stitch Guide

ASSEMBLING

Gather the neck edge of the body and insert the cotter pin from the head. Draw in the gathering thread tightly around the pin and tie off. Attach a disc and washer to the cotter pin inside the body, then turn down the ends of the pin using the long-nose pliers. Stuff paw and foot pads in the limbs firmly. Insert the joints and assemble in the same way as before. Complete stuffing the limbs, stuffing firmly around the joints then ladder-stitch the openings closed. Stuff the body firmly, especially around the joints and the neck, and close the opening. You may wish to fill the middle of the body with pellets for a floppier bear, however, this is not suitable for a child's toy.

EYES

Using glass-headed pins, locate the desired position for the eyes and ears, then make a small eye hole with the awl. Push the awl diagonally across from the eye position to the opposite ear position, but do not exit at this point. With pliers, squeeze the wire loops on the eyes till they are almost flat. Using about 1m of strong thread folded in half, insert the two ends through the wire loop and tie a knot in the middle of the thread. Thread a doll needle with two of these threads, then insert into one

eye hole. Take the needle through the head, following the previously created channel, coming out at the opposite ear position. Thread the remaining two threads on the prepared eye through the same channel, exiting about 1mm from the first threads. Pull the threads tightly to sink the eye into the head and knot the ends several times. Take all the ends through the head to the opposite ear position, pull tight and snip off ends. Repeat for the other eye. Both knots will be concealed when the ears are stitched in place.

EARS

Pinch the fabric on each side of the base seam, causing the ear to form a curve which will fit nicely onto the head. Pin the ear into position and ladder-stitch in place with the strong thread. Tuck in the ends into to hide the raw edges. ❁

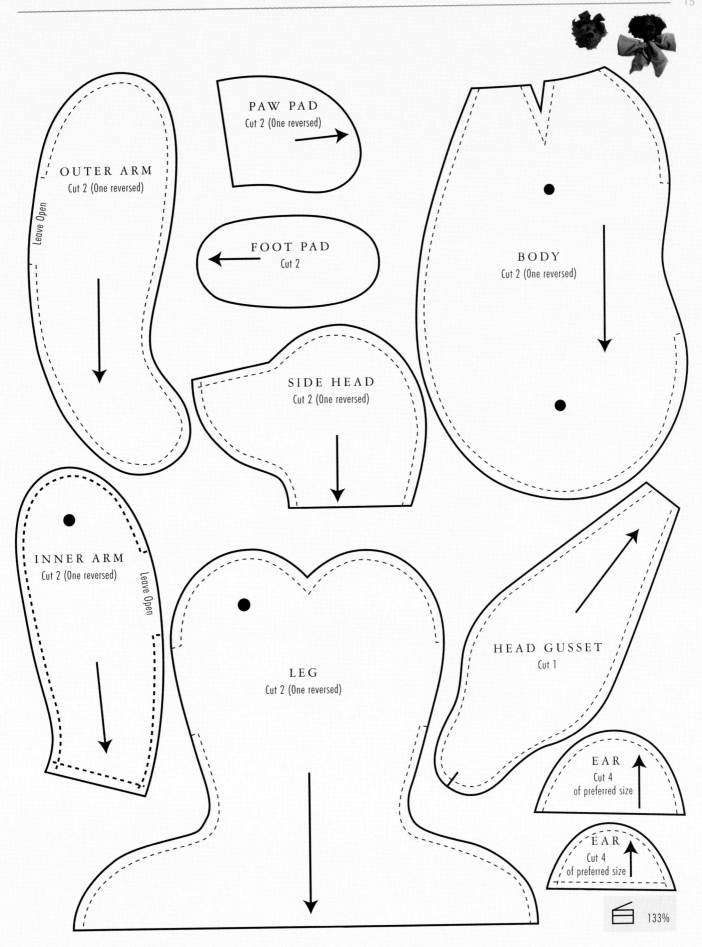

PAW PAD
Cut 2 (One reversed)

OUTER ARM
Cut 2 (One reversed)

Leave Open

FOOT PAD
Cut 2

BODY
Cut 2 (One reversed)

SIDE HEAD
Cut 2 (One reversed)

INNER ARM
Cut 2 (One reversed)

Leave Open

HEAD GUSSET
Cut 1

LEG
Cut 2 (One reversed)

EAR
Cut 4
of preferred size

EAR
Cut 4
of preferred size

133%

Koala Teddy

This Aussie fellow is designed by Romy Roeder of Vagabond Bears.
Fully jointed, this little antipodean battler will steal your heart.

PREPARATION

Trace the pattern carefully onto paper and cut out. Pin and mark the pieces onto the wrong side of fabric using a fine-tipped pen – be sure to transfer all markings and cut out with small scissors, taking care not to cut the fur. A 3mm seam allowance is included in the pattern.

STITCHING

Head: Firstly pin, oversew and backstitch all the darts marked on the head pieces. Pin the two side pieces together with the right sides facing from neck to nose. Pin the side pieces to the head gusset. Oversew all the pinned raw edges, leaving the bottom of the neck open. Backstitch or machine-stitch the oversewn edges. Turn right side out.

Body: Pin all the body parts together, oversew all pinned edges and leave the top open for the neck joint, just big enough for a bolt to fit through. Leave opening at the back as marked. Backstitch or machine-stitch, turning the right side out through the back opening.

Arms: Position and pin Koala's felt paws to his wrist, oversewing the edges and then backstitch or machine-stitch. Pin the whole arm together, with right sides in, leaving an opening as marked. Oversew pinned edges, backstitch or machine-stitch. Turn right side out and repeat on other arm.

Legs: Pin the leg pieces together with the right sides facing, leaving the opening as marked. Oversew the edges, then backstitch or machine-stitch. Pin in the felt foot pad, oversew the pinned edges using back stitch or machine-stitch. Turn right side out. Repeat for the other leg.

Ears: Pin the ear parts together with right sides facing, oversew the curved edges using backstitching or machine-stitching. Turn the right sides out and sew up the bottom opening with a running stitch.

FINISHING HEAD

Head: Using polyester stuffing starting at the nose, fill firmly, using a small amount of fibre at a time and using the stuffing tool when needed. When the head is firmly filled, insert a bolt through one of the neck discs and set into head/neck opening, with bolt end sticking out of the neck. Sew running stitch in strong cotton, doubled, around the lower neckline and draw closed around the bolt. Do this twice, secure with double knot and cut.

Ears: Pin ears on to the head in a position that is most pleasing to you. First sew along one side, and then on other side to secure them to the head.

Eyes: Find the desired position of the eyes and mark with pins. Thread eye onto a long piece of strong thread or dental floss, secure with a slip knot, then place thread through the doll needle. Secure the eye by drawing the thread diagonally through to the back of the head, exiting at the neck joint in the centre of the head. Repeat with the other end of the thread, exiting next to the first thread. Knot these long strands together, pulling the eye firmly into the head. Fasten off with a double knot, bury the knot into the head, and repeat with his second eye.

Nose: Pin black felt nose to the face, referring to the photo for correct positioning and taking care to push back the fur. You can also use a little bit of polyester filling or double thickness of felt to achieve the right look. Using the embroidery thread, sew the nose in place with tiny stitches.

FINISHED SIZE

• Approximately 32cm (12$\frac{1}{2}$in)

MATERIALS

• 23cm x 40cm (9in x 16in) brown/grey mohair, 2cm ($\frac{7}{8}$in) pile

• 23cm x 23cm (9in x 9in) white mohair, 2cm ($\frac{7}{8}$in) pile

• Small piece black felt for nose.

• Felt to match mohair for paw pads

• Black Perlé embroidery cotton for claws and mouth stitching

• 1 pair 11-12mm ($\frac{1}{2}$in) brown or black glass eyes

• 2 x 30mm (1$\frac{1}{4}$in) discs for neck

• 8 x 40mm (1$\frac{1}{2}$in) discs

• 5 x 20mm ($\frac{3}{4}$in) long bolts with matching washers and nuts

• Strong sewing cotton

• Doll needle

• Sharp scissors

• Polyester stuffing

• Awl

• Stuffing tool

• 2 spanners

• Fine felt-tip pen

• Gumnuts to attach to teddy

• General sewing requirements

carefully pierce a hole for the joint. Insert the bolt through the arm hole, then find the joint holes on the upper body, making a corresponding hole with the awl. Use the same procedure as described for the neck joint, repeat with the other arm, taking care to keep the arms even.

Legs: Use the same procedure as for the arms. Remembering to keep the joints tight.

JOINTING AND STUFFING

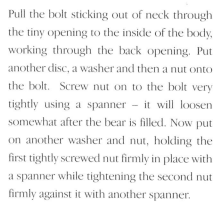

Pull the bolt sticking out of neck through the tiny opening to the inside of the body, working through the back opening. Put another disc, a washer and then a nut onto the bolt. Screw nut on to the bolt very tightly using a spanner – it will loosen somewhat after the bear is filled. Now put on another washer and nut, holding the first tightly screwed nut firmly in place with a spanner while tightening the second nut firmly against it with another spanner.

Arms: Begin stuffing the arms by inserting small amounts of stuffing into the paws and fill arm to about halfway. Insert the bolt through one of the arm discs and place inside the arm. Find the correct position for the joint on the inside top of the arm. Using the awl,

FILLING

Stuff your koala as firmly as you prefer, using only small amounts of polyester filling at a time and using the stuffing tool to fill all corners. Close the openings with Ladder Stitch.

FINISHING

❖

Using the same embroidery thread as for the mouth, sew on the claws with blanket stitches or equivalent.

To get that Aussie look, sew or glue gumnuts, Australian flags or other Aussie paraphernalia to Koala's neck or chest.❈

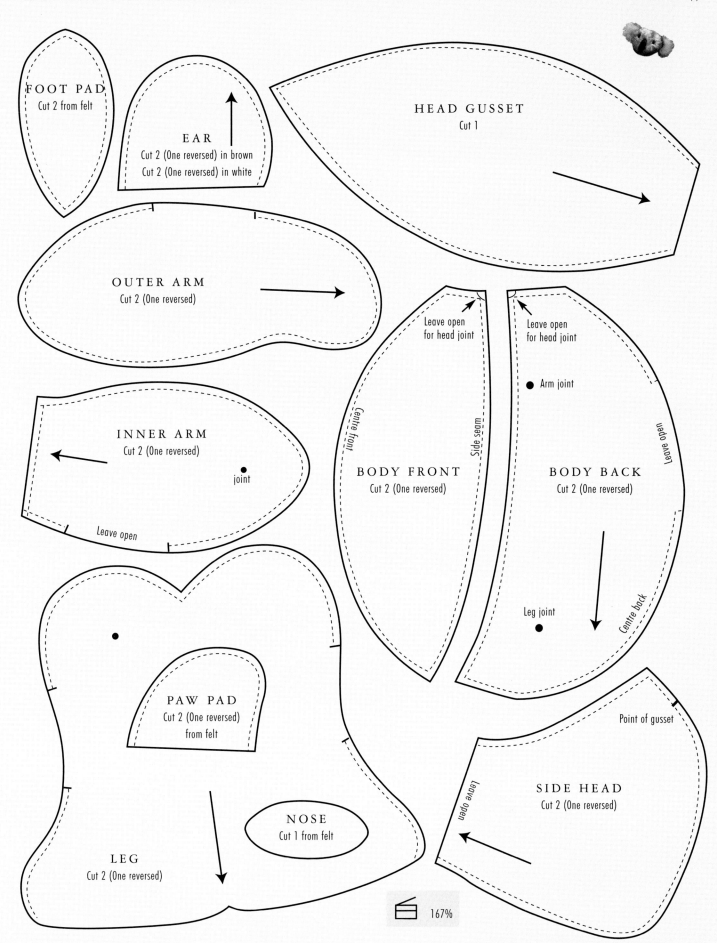

FOOT PAD
Cut 2 from felt

EAR
Cut 2 (One reversed) in brown
Cut 2 (One reversed) in white

HEAD GUSSET
Cut 1

OUTER ARM
Cut 2 (One reversed)

Leave open
for head joint

Leave open
for head joint

Arm joint

Centre front

Side seam

Leave open

INNER ARM
Cut 2 (One reversed)

joint

BODY FRONT
Cut 2 (One reversed)

BODY BACK
Cut 2 (One reversed)

Leave open

Centre back

Leg joint

PAW PAD
Cut 2 (One reversed)
from felt

Point of gusset

Leave open

SIDE HEAD
Cut 2 (One reversed)

LEG
Cut 2 (One reversed)

NOSE
Cut 1 from felt

167%

Teddy Hug-me-Tight

Teddy Hug-me-Tight, by Margaret Ann Mann, has her own little teddy to hug and patchwork quilt to keep her snug. A wire armature means she can wrap her arms around her little toy.

PREPARATION

❖

Read instructions carefully before you begin. The head gusset is cut the opposite way to the norm so the fur flows downwards, giving a fringe effect. Transfer pattern onto firm cardboard and trace onto back of fabric. The arrows on the pattern should follow the direction of the fur pile. Transfer all markings and reverse pattern pieces where necessary. Pin and overcast edges, pushing fur away from the stitching line, then backstitch using the Dual Duty Plus hand-quilting thread. A 6mm seam allowance is included in the pattern.

STITCHING THE BEAR

❖

Head: With side head pieces right sides together, sew from the tip of the nose down to the neck. Pin head gusset into place matching the nose point to the seam and easing where necessary. Stitch into place.

Body: Pin, then stitch the body pieces together, leaving openings at the back and the neck joint as indicated. Make joint holes with an awl where marked, then turn right side out.

Limbs: Sew arms, leaving openings where indicated, then make joint holes on the inner arms. Sew legs, again leaving openings where indicated. Match centre marks on foot pads to the leg seams, and pin, then stitch into place.

Ears: Stitch ears as marked on pattern and turn right side out. Fold in raw edges and oversew.

JOINTING AND STUFFING

❖

With a strong upholstery thread, run a gathering stitch around the neck edge of both head and body, leaving tails of thread to pull up. Stuff head firmly, paying special attention to the snout which must be quite firm for the nose to be embroidered satisfactorily.

Continue stuffing the rest of the head, checking from all angles to ensure it is evenly stuffed. Attach a washer and disc to the bolt and insert into head opening, then draw the gathering thread tight around the end of the bolt, knot three times and hide the thread in the neck area.

Insert head bolt into body neck opening and attach a disc, washer and locknut. Tighten with screwdriver and pliers. Place six drops of Supa-glue onto the nut and washer and leave to dry. Stuff shoulders and base of body firmly and place a fine layer over the tummy seam. Pour in six teaspoons of glass pellets if desired, then add more polyester stuffing and close with Ladder Stitch.

The limb joints are assembled in the limbs, then inserted into the appropriate holes in the body. If you are using armature, follow the directions on the pack. It should be at least 2cm shorter than the length from the shoulder joint to the tip of the paw to enable you to cover the end of the armature wire with stuffing once it is in place.

Assemble joints as before and insert into limb, then into body. Before tightening, ensure the limbs are facing in the right direction. Joints should be tightened so they can just move as they will loosen when the bear is stuffed.

FINISHED SIZE

- 25cm (10in)

MATERIALS

- 25cm x 65cm (10in x 26in) sparse distressed mohair with 2cm (³/₄in) pile
- 15cm (6in) square of felt for foot pads and small teddy
- Small pieces of fabric for quilt
- Size 9 glass or boot-button eyes
- Four sets of 20mm (³/₄in) wooden discs, nuts and bolts for arms and legs
- Pair of wooden discs plus one Zenith ⁵/₃₂in x 1in bolt and nut for neck (sold in packets of 8)
- Pack of 100mm Teddy Bear Armature with instructions
- Extra-strong Dual Duty Plus hand-quilting thread in a matching colour
- Upholstery thread in a matching colour for seams
- DMC Perlé cotton for nose in colour of choice
- Dental floss
- 10-15cm (4-6in) doll needle
- Small bag polyester filling
- 6 teaspoons of small glass or plastic pellets (see note)
- Chopstick or stuffing tool
- Needle-nose pliers
- Medium Phillip's head screwdriver
- Good quality, sharp pointed scissors for cutting fur
- Marker pen
- General sewing requirements

Note: If this bear is to be given to a baby or small child, we recommend you do not use glass or plastic pellets to fill the bears.

NOSE

Snip the fur from a small triangular area at the point of the snout so you can stitch the nose at the end of the gusset. Remember, noses take practice and if you aren't satisfied with your effort, unpick carefully and re-stitch.

When you finish stitching the nose, bring the needle out at the centre seam at the base of the nose, select a mouth shape from our suggestions and stitch accordingly. Hide ends of threads in the head near the neck.

EYES

The usual position for a bear's eyes is where the snout rises to form the brow. Flatten the wire loop at the back of each glass eye with pliers until it is approximately the size of the eye of a darning needle. Don't do this if you decide to use boot-button eyes as the eye could crack.

When you are happy with the eye placement, make a hole with an awl or knitting needle, but never pierce the seam. Thread approximately 50cm (20in) of dental floss through the loop at the back of each eye and secure with a slip-knot. Thread the ends through your long doll needle. Insert each eye separately on a slight diagonal, bringing the needle out at the centre-back of the head, near the neck joint. Pull threads very firmly to sink the eyes. Knot threads three times, hide the floss back into the head and snip off the ends.

EARS

Pin the ears to your bear's head in the position you prefer. Curve the ears forward slightly and ladder-stitch in place.

SMALL TEDDY

This little teddy is made from felt, sewn together with a buttonhole stitch and very lightly stuffed. If desired you can embroider the eyes and nose with embroidery thread.

QUILT

The fabric used for the little quilt is a patchwork design which has been tea-dyed for an aged look, however, you can use any fabric you desire. The quilt measures 16cm x 20cm (6$\frac{1}{4}$in x 8in) and has a thin layer of batting and calico backing. It has been outline-quilted around the design and embroidered with some words of wisdom.

Choose a charm or other keep sake for your bear's wrist, brush her gently and wrap her arms around her teddy and quilt.❊

Nutmeg

Nutmeg, by Adele Rowe from The Serendipity Collection,
is a very huggable, fully jointed bear with
armature so he can be easily posed.

PREPARATIONS

❖

Trace pattern to either template plastic or Vilene, transferring all markings, then cut out and trace to the back of your fabric. Note the position of openings on legs and arms located at the top to make it easier to insert armature. Before cutting fabric, check that all pieces have been transferred. Paws and pads can be in suede, wool felt or fabric used for miniature bears. Carefully cut out pattern pieces from fabric with sharp embroidery scissors. Use only the tips of the scissors and cut backing of fabric, not the fur. You may wish to accurately trim the fur from the seam allowance to reduce bulk and make seams less visible on the finished bear. To help prevent fraying, iron fabric stabiliser to the openings. Pin and overcast all seams before stitching. Mark all joints and eye positions from the fur side using contrasting thread.

HEAD

❖

Place side head pieces together with right sides together and stitch from nose to neck. Place centre front seam and secure in place with three or four stitches. Starting from centre front, pin gusset in position, working around the back of the head and finishing at the neck. Overcast and stitch from the neck to the nose, returning to the neck. Turn right side out and stuff firmly with small pieces of filling. Using extra-strong thread doubled, run a gathering thread around the base of the neck, leaving a 4in tail at each end. Attach a metal washer and felt disc into the head, then pull gathering thread very tightly around split pin. Tie knot and lose the thread in the head before cutting.

BODY

❖

Pin and sew darts, slit with sharp scissors as indicated on pattern and lay flat. Pin and sew body pieces together with right sides facing, leaving openings as marked. Using extra-strong thread doubled, run a gathering stitch around the top of the body using the same method as for the head. Pull in tightly and knot. Cut thread leaving two inch tails inside the body. Turn body right side out and leave aside.

ARMS

❖

Sew paw pads to inner arms. Match inner arm to outer arm and sew together. Repeat for other arm. Openings can be changed to the side if you are not using armature.

LEGS

❖

Match inner and outer leg pieces, leaving openings as marked. Again, if you are not using armature, the openings can be changed to the middle of the back of the leg. Match centre front of foot pad to toe of leg, then overcast and stitch in position. Repeat for other leg.

JOINTING AND FILLING

❖

With armature: armature can be used in either the arms or legs, or both, however, it shouldn't press tightly against the fabric. To work out the length of the armature required, measure from the leg or arm joint to just below the wrist or

FINISHED SIZE

40cm (16in)

MATERIALS

• 25cm (^{1}/$_4$yd) mohair or acrylic fabric

• 15cm (6in) square of suede, felt of mini bear fabric for paw pads

• For armature jointing you will need: 6 x 45mm (1^3/$_4$in) wooden discs for arms and head, 4 x 50mm (2in) wooden discs for legs, 5x40mm (1^1/$_2$in) split pins and 5 metal washers, 11 links of plastic armature for each arm, 10 links of plastic armature for each leg

• For jointing without armature you will need: Wooden discs as above 40mm (1^1/$_2$in) split pin, 4 x 35mm (1^1/$_4$in) split pins, Washers or 5 locknuts, 5 hex screws and washers

• 11mm (^{3}/$_8$in) glass eyes or 12mm (^{1}/$_2$in) safety eyes

• Polyester filling

• No 8 DMC Perlé cotton in dark brown for nose

• Matching sewing thread

• Strong thread

• Synthetic gut

• Doll needles

• Iron-on fabric stabiliser (optional)

• Awl or knitting needle

• Fine marking pen

• Template plastic or Vilene for tracing pattern

• Ring spanner or needle-nose pliers

• General sewing requirements

suitable for bears with armature because of the weight of the pellets. They also substantially lessen the bear's poseability.

EARS

Place ears together with right sides facing and stitch around the curved edge and the outer edge of the base. Trim corners, turn right side out, then close with Ladder Stitch. Pin ears into position using our bear as a guide and ladder-stitch firmly into place.

EYES

Using an awl, make holes for the eyes. Cut synthetic gut into required length and split into four or five widths. take one length and fold in half, then take the loop of the gut through the loop at the back of the eye. Feed the tails of the gut onto a large doll needle and insert into the eye hole, coming out at the lowest point possible in the centre back of the head. Repeat for the other eye, bring the needle out as close as possible to the first threads. ensure the eyes are even and firmly indented, then knot all the threads together. Lose the ends of the thread into the head.

FINISHING

The muzzle fur can be left as is or shaved. Look at magazines and books to get inspiration and develop your own style. Embroider the nose with Perlé cotton. Bring the thread up from the side of the head into the centre of the nose position

ankle. To add or remove inks, use armature pliers. Add a link by inserting the ball of the link to the lip side of the pliers. Add the socket to the other side of the pliers, then squeeze pliers closed, causing the links to pop together. To remove links, reverse this method. For our bear, we used 40mm split pins. The rounded head of the split pin has been enlarged using needle-nose pliers, then shaped around the top link of he armature. A disc is then attached to the pin and the joint is finished in the usual manner. Before jointing, stuff paws and foot pads, being careful not to stuff too tightly so as to restrict the movement of the armature. Prepare the armature as above, place into arm or leg from the top opening, then complete the jointing. Continue stuffing the limbs, then close the openings with ladder stitch.

The body should be filled with the same consistency and the opening closed with Ladder Stitch. Pellet filling is not

and make a small back stitch to secure. Work from the centre out to one side, using a straight, even Satin Stitch. Go back to the centre and work out to the other side. Work mouth with straight stitches, taking care not to pull stitches too tightly. Finish off with a small backstitch and lose the thread inside the head.❄

Lil' Sailor

*Ship ahoy! Lil' Sailor sits on the shore with her jaunty sailor's cap and bib,
ready to sail the seven seas. This darling little bear was designed
by Carlene Hughes. Her pattern and instructions were kindly given
to us by Helen Yasmine of Dolls in the Attic and Bears Too.*

PREPARATION

Trace the pattern pieces onto interfacing and cut out. Place the pieces on the back of the appropriate fabrics and trace around with a fabric pen. Cut the body, head, ears and limbs from the gold fur fabric. Cut the foot pads from the gold Ultrasuede and the hat and collar from the white fur fabric. Hand sew your bear using either a Blanket Stitch or a Back Stitch.

BODY AND HEAD

With right sides facing, pin, then stitch the body pieces together, leaving the neck edge open. Using the blunt end of the bamboo stick, slowly and carefully turn to the right side. Stuff the body. Run a gathering stitch around the neck edge, pull up tightly and secure. With right sides facing, pin, then stitch the side-head pieces together, stitching from A to B. Match the A on the head gusset with the A on the side-head pieces. Stitch from the nose to the back of the neck. Starting at the nose point (A), repeat for the other side of the head gusset. Carefully turn to the right side. Stuff, carefully moulding the shape of the face as you work. Run a gathering stitch around the neck edge, pull up tightly and secure.

EAR AND FACE

With right sides together, stitch around the curved edge of the ear, leaving the base open. Turn to the right side and over stitch the opening. Attach the ear to the head with a Ladder Stitch.

To attach the eyes, take a double strand of thread from the back of the neck to the selected position of the eyes. Thread on an eye and take the needle back through the head to the back of the neck. Pull on both strands of double thread to deeply set in the eye. Tie off the threads and repeat for the other eye. Using Perlé thread and following the photographs, stitch the nose in Satin Stitch from the mouth by stitching an inverted Y with Perlé thread.

ARMS AND LEGS

Arms: With right sides together, stitch around the arms, leaving the opening where marked. Turn to the right side and stuff firmly. Close the opening with a Ladder Stitch.

Legs: With right sides facing, stitch from the heel up to the opening, then from the toe around to the opening. Carefully stitch the foot pads into place. Turn to the right side and stuff firmly . The opening is closed using a Ladder Stitch.

Use Perlé thread to stitch three claws on both arms and legs. Lose the ends of the thread inside the limbs.

ASSEMBLING THE BEAR

Join the head to the body using a firm Ladder Stitch. To attach the arms, take a long double strand of thread through the inside arm to the outside of the arm then return through the same hole. Take the thread through the body and arm at the opposite side. Repeat this four or five times, pulling the thread tightly each time.

Note: It is important to attach as closely as possible through the same

FINISHED SIZE

5cm (2in) sitting

MATERIALS

- 12.5cm (5in) square of gold fur fabric
- 7.5cm (3in) square of white fur fabric
- Scrap of gold Ultrasuede for foot pads
- Two black onyx eyes
- Perlé thread for nose and claws
- Matching sewing threads
- Polyester fibrefil
- Small piece of thin ribbon
- Small piece of braid
- Scrap of pink material for pompom
- Bamboo stick or skewer
- Tacky craft glue
- Fabric pen

hole, or limbs will not turn properly. Keep checking that they turn freely, but firmly, each time you pass the needle through the limb.

To finish, take the thread through the body, tie a strong knot against the body, re-thread the needle and sink the knot into the body. Attach the legs in the same manner as for the arms.

HAT AND COLLAR

❖

With the right sides together, stitch around the hat top, leaving an opening for turning. Turn to the right side and close the opening with a Ladder Stitch. Stitch the short ends of the hat side together, and turn to the right side. Using a small Slip Stitch, attach the hat side to

the hat top. position the hat on Lil' Sailor's head and slip-stitch into place. Trim the hat with ribbon or braid, gluing into place. Add a pompom to the top. To make the pompom, cut a small circle from the pink fabric scrap. Gather around the outside edge. Fill with a small amount of stuffing, pull up the gathers tightly and secure. Place the collar pieces together, right sides facing. Stitch around the edges, leaving the opening for turning where shown. Very carefully turn to the right side. Close the opening with a Ladder Stitch. Attach to the bear by tacking the ends together at the front, then gluing down at the front and back with a small amount of tacky glue. Make a small ribbon bow and attach to the front of the collar. Your Lil' Sailor is ready for the high seas! You could always make her a boy partner by simply changing the trimmings to blue.❁

Lil' Sailor Pattern

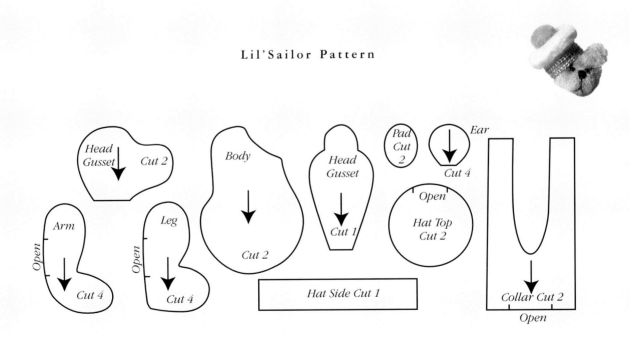

Head Gusset Cut 2

Arm Open Cut 4

Leg Open Cut 4

Body Cut 2

Head Gusset Cut 1

Pad Cut 2

Ear Cut 4

Open Hat Top Cut 2

Hat Side Cut 1

Collar Cut 2 Open

Actual size

Joffa and Byron

Although they may be lifelike grizzlies, these winsome bears are as gentle as lambs. Designed by Pam Campbell of Campbell Bears, Joffa is made from brown-tipped mohair, while Byron is made from cream woven-backed acrylic fur.

PREPARATION

If machine-sewing set your machine to a stitch length of approximately 1.5.

If you have trouble inserting the foot pads, snip into the seam allowance on the lower edge of the leg before pinning the pads on. This will help ease the curve of the paw pad. A seam allowance of 6mm has been included in the pattern.

BODY AND HEAD

Pin darts on the head and body and sew. Use your bodkin to flip out any fur caught between the seams.(This needs to be done on all seams). Place the side head pieces with right sides together. Sew from nose to chin (A to B). Stitch again for extra strength.

With right sides together, insert the head gusset between the two side head pieces, matching C to A. Pin and sew, remembering to leave an opening if you are using locknut joints. Place the ear pieces in pairs with right sides together. Sew around the curved edges and turn. Place the body halves with right sides together and sew, leaving an opening for turning and stuffing. Leave a space at the neck just large enough for a bolt or cotter pin to fit through.

LIMBS

Fold arms in half with right side facing and stitch, leaving an opening for the stuffing.

With right sides facing, fold leg pieces in half. Leave an opening for stuffing. Clip the fur of the paw pads, then pin to the bottom of the legs with right sides

together and sew. Use the awl to make joint holes in the limbs where marked. Turn all limbs right side out and pick out any fur trapped in the seams.

STUFFING AND JOINTING

Stuff the head firmly, using the stuffing tool and small a amount of soft stuffing. Mould the nose as you stuff it. Load a bolt or cotter pin with a matching washer and a 30m disc. Insert disc into the neck of the head, leaving the end of the bolt protruding. Using strong thread, sew a running stitch around the base of the head, 6mm from the edge. Pull firmly to gather the neck and secure. Fill the feet and paws with small amounts of stuffing. Insert the cotter pin or bolts which have been loaded with the matching discs and the washer, into the joint marks in the limbs. Push bolts or pin through the corresponding joint holes in the body. Working through the body opening, place the matching disc, washer and locknut onto the bolt and tighten with a screwdriver and ring spanner.

If using a cotter pin, place the matching wooden disc and the metal washer over the pin and secure by rolling over the ends of the pin with the pliers. Attach the head by inserting the protruding bolt or pin through the small opening in body neck. Work through the body opening and secure in the same manner as for the limbs.

Stuff body, limbs and head firmly, closing all openings with a strong Ladder Stitch.

FINISHED SIZE:

- 30cm (12in)

MATERIALS:

- 85cm x 30cm (33½in x 12in) acrylic or mohair fur
- 2 x 9mm (³/₈in) glass eyes
- Strong sewing thread
- Black or brown Perlé thread
- 2 x 35mm (1½in) wooden discs for legs
- 3 x 30mm (1¼in) wooden discs for arms and head
- Matching cotter pins or locknuts, washers and bolts
- Polyester stuffing
- Dental floss
- Lightweight cardboard
- Screwdriver and ring spanner(if using locknuts)
- Fine, black waterproof marking pen
- Awl or metal knitting needle
- Doll needle
- Stuffing tool
- Sharp scissors
- Bodkin or fine Knitting needle
- Water-soluble pen (optional)
- Round-nosed pliers
- General sewing requirements

FINISHING YOUR BEAR

Trim the fur on the nose muzzle very carefully, using sharp scissors, until you have achieved the desired effect. Embroider the nose with even Satin Stitches using the Perlé thread It may help to draw an outline of the nose and mouth on the bear first using a water-soluble pen, and use this as a stitch guide. Pam often likes to embroider beautiful heart-shape noses on her bears to give them a very individual look. Her method produces a very neat finish, however, you will still achieve a pleasing result by choosing a simpler shape if you are not an experienced embroiderer.

Using the same thread, stitch an inverted Y underneath the nose. Position the eyes and mark with a pin. (You can check the position by looking at the bear in the mirror.) Use an awl to mark holes in the eye position. thread a double strand of dental floss through the eye loop and thread all four strands on a long doll needle. Insert the needle through the eye hole and come out at the base of the neck, next to the neck joint. Leave

the thread hanging and repeat with the other eye, coming out at the same spot. Push the eyes in hard with your thumbs and pull the threads firmly to sink the eyes, tying off securely. Hide the loose ends by threading them back into the bear's head.

Fold the lower edge of the ears under 6mm and stitch with dental floss or strong thread, leaving the end hanging. Position the ears on the head and ladder-stitch them in place.

Brush the fur out of all seams.❁

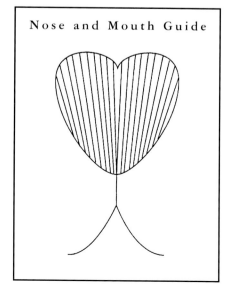

Nose and Mouth Guide

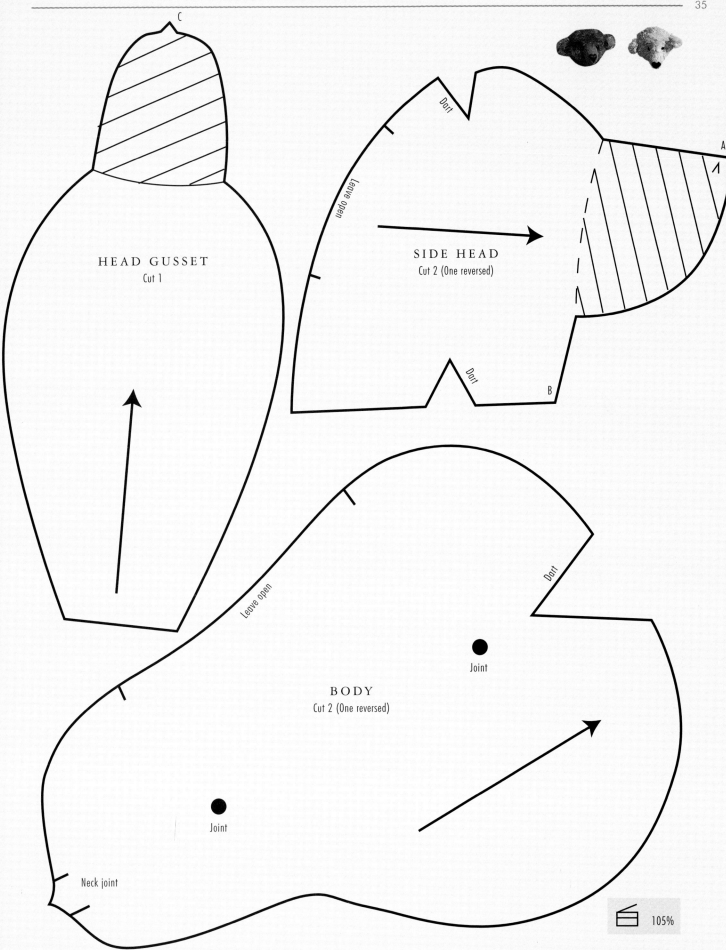

C

HEAD GUSSET
Cut 1

Dart

Leave open

SIDE HEAD
Cut 2 (One reversed)

A

Dart

B

Leave open

Dart

Joint

BODY
Cut 2 (One reversed)

Joint

Neck joint

105%

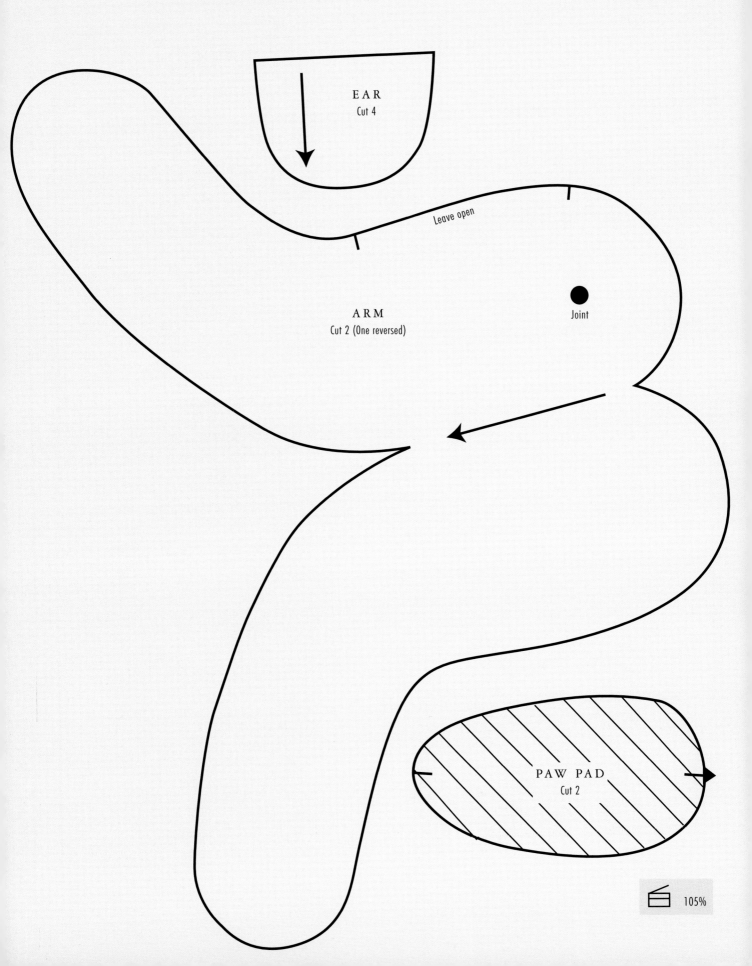

EAR
Cut 4

Leave open

ARM
Cut 2 (One reversed)

Joint

PAW PAD
Cut 2

105%

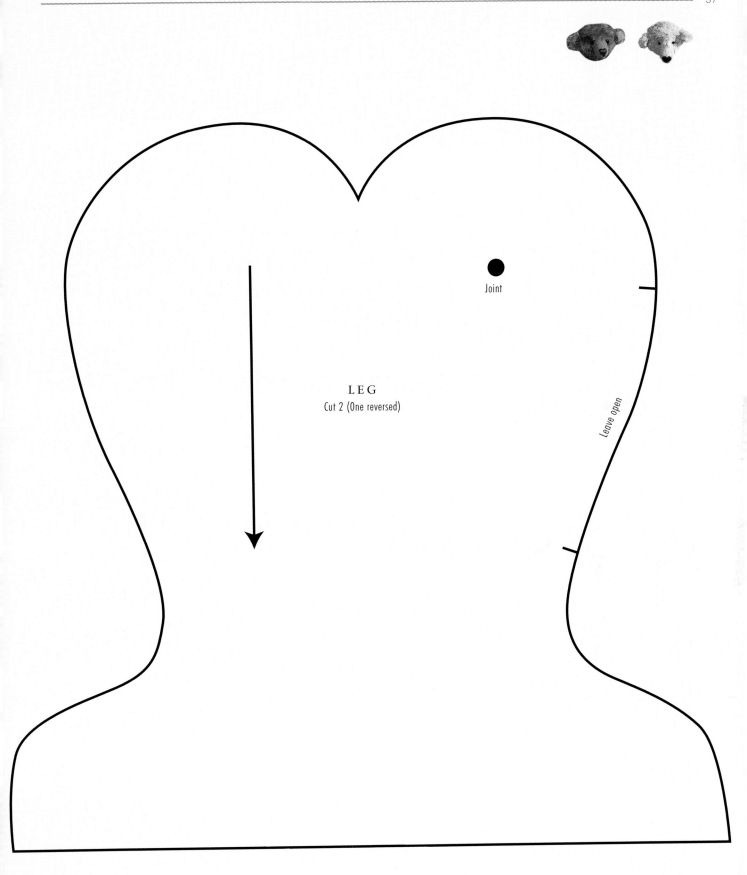

Joint

LEG
Cut 2 (One reversed)

Leave open

105%

Emma-Louise

Emma-Louise loves nothing better than to stitch her projects under a shady tree. Designed by Melody Daly, her old-world looks are enhanced by spraying her with a light mist of Parisian essence.

PREPARATION

❖

Read all instructions thoroughly before starting. Copy the pattern and paste onto cardboard. Position the head, head gusset, ears, body, arms, legs and foot pad pieces on the cotton batting and trace around the pattern pieces, transferring all markings. Because this fabric has no grain, pattern pieces can be positioned to fit, but the textures of each side are different, so be sure to reverse pieces as indicated. Cut out the nose from the brown felt. Cut the pinafore bodice and a 24cm x 115cm rectangle for the skirt from fabric A.

Cut the bloomers from fabric B and the blouse from fabric C. A seam allowance of 5mm is included in the pattern.

The body seams should be pinned and tacked with an overcast stitch, then either machine-stitched or back-stitched. Use single thread for overcasting and double thread for back-stitching. The clothing should be pinned and machine-stitched.

STITCHING

❖

Head: Place the side head pieces right sides together and stitch from the tip of the nose (point B) to the neck edge (point A). Fold the head gusset in half and pinch to form a crease down the centre at B. Line up this crease with the centre front seam and stitch from point B to point C on one side of the nose, repeating on the other side. then stitch from point C to point D on both side head pieces. Turn head right side out.

Ears: With the right sides facing, fold the ear piece in half and stitch around the curved seamline. Carefully cut a slit where indicated on the pattern piece and turn right side out. Using dental floss,

sew the slit closed with ladder stitch, pulling the thread tightly so the fabric gathers slightly. Leave thread attached to secure the ears to the head at a later stage. Repeat with the other ear.

Arms: Place the two arm pieces right sides together, stitch around the seamline and turn right side out.

ASSEMBLING

❖

Body: Stuff the body firmly, adding small amounts of stuffing at a time and making sure not to stretch the cotton batting out of shape.

Legs: Stuff the legs firmly up to the line marked on the pattern. Sew across this line with back stitch to form the knee. Insert the legs into the opening at the bottom of the body and pin into position. Sew the legs into place with a small Ladder Stitch, ensuring the entire gap is closed. Using two strands of brown cotton, sew around the bottom of the feet with a large straight stitch or a 'naive' stitch. Make a few naive stitches on one leg just above the ankle, referring to the photo for detail.

Arms: Using the stuffing tool, stuff the arms firmly, taking care not to overstuff. Attach the arms to the body at the shoulders with a Ladder Stitch. Stitch the paws with a naive stitch using two strands of brown stranded cotton.

Head: Again using small amounts of stuffing at a time, stuff the head firmly, making sure you fill the nose. Attach the head to the body by inserting the top of the body into the gap at the neck of the head. Sew in place with Ladder Stitch using dental floss. With the long thread left attached to the ears, sew the ears onto the head with Ladder Stitch and using the placement marks as a guide. Tie off remaining thread securely.

Eyes: Position the eyes and make

MATERIALS

- 50cm x 90cm (¹/₂yd x 35¹/₂in) cotton batting
- 40cm x 115cm (³/₈yd x 45in) fabric for pinafore (fabric A)
- 30cm x 115 (¹/₃yd x 45in) fabric for bloomers (fabric B)
- 20cm x 115cm (¹/₄yd x 45in) fabric for shirt (fabric C)
- 11mm (³/₈in) glass eyes
- Scrap of brown felt for nose
- Dental floss
- Matching sewing thread
- Brown Perlé thread for mouth
- Brown stranded cotton for stitching around paws
- Polyester stuffing
- Stuffing tool or chopstick
- Doll needle
- Awl
- Fine-tip pen
- 6 small buttons
- 9cm (3¹/₂in) plastic woodgrain embroidery hoop
- Scraps of materials for hearts on skirt
- Small scrap of calico
- Parisian essence
- Small refillable spray bottle
- Contrasting stranded cotton thread
- Small charm and chain or thread
- Vliesofix
- Tracing paper
- cardboard
- General sewing requirements

small holes with the awl, taking care not to tear the fabric. Thread an eye with dental floss, then thread both ends of the floss through a doll needle. Insert the needle into the eye hole and bring it out at the base at the rear of the head. Repeat with the other eye. Pull firmly on the threads to sink the eyes. Tie the threads together a number of times and end off.

Nose: Using the photograph as a guide, place the felt nose into position and attach with small stitches. Using Perlé thread, sew the mouth with straight stitches.

CLOTHING

Bloomers: With right sides together, fold over each pant leg piece and sew from point A to point B as marked on the pattern. Turn one leg right side out and insert this leg into the other leg so the right sides are together. Sew crotch from point C down to A and up to C on the other side. Turn right side out and place the bloomers on your bear. Fold over the top edge and sew a running stitch around the top of the bloomers. Use three strands of contrasting stranded cotton, starting at the middle front and leaving the ends of the thread hanging. Draw the ends of the thread together, tie a knot to form a bow. Turn under the raw edges at the bottom of each leg and, using the same method as described for the waistband, gather and make a bow in the middle of each pant leg.

Blouse: Place the two blouse pieces right sides together and sew along the shoulder seams, leaving neck open as indicated on the pattern. Sew under the arms and side seams. Turn right side out and place the blouse on your bear. Tuck under the raw edges around the neck, and sew using Ladder Stitch and matching

thread. Fold under the edges of the bottom of each sleeve and sew a running stitch around the edge using three strands of contrasting cotton. Tie a bow as described previously. Fold under the lower edge of the blouse and sew a running stitch around the edge, again using three strands of cotton.

Pinafore: Place the two pinafore bodice pieces right sides together and sew along the seamlines, leaving the lower edge open. Clip the corners and turn right side out.

Fold the bodice into a circular shape, overlapping the right front on the left by one centimetre. Stitch this overlap closed along the lower edge using an overcast stitch. With right sides together, sew the skirt together along the centre back seam. Sew the top of the skirt with a running stitch, then gather to fit the bodice. Pin, then sew the skirt to the bodice, placing the skirt seam at the centre back of the pinafore.

Cut the two heart shapes out of Vliesofix, leaving 1cm around each heart. Iron each heart, paper side up, onto the wrong side of the fabric you will be using for the hearts and cut out. Peel off the paper from the smaller heart and iron it onto the larger heart. Peel off remaining paper and iron hearts onto the pinafore skirt, using the photograph as a guide to positioning. Using two strands of contrasting cotton, sew around the larger heart with naive stitch.

Fray a 1cm fringe around the bottom edge of the skirt. Place the pinafore on your bear. Overlap the pinafore shoulder pieces by 1cm and join each strap by sewing on a button, using four strands of contrasting stranded cotton.

Tie a knot on top of each button. Cut off the threads, leaving 1cm to fluff out. Attach three buttons down the front of the pinafore and one button to the heart motif using the same method.

FINISHING TOUCHES

Tear a strip of fabric approximately 4cm wide and tie it around Emma-Louise's head in a bow. Thread the charm onto a chain or heavy cotton thread and place around your bear's neck. Insert a small piece of calico into the embroidery hoop. Attach a small motif from one of your fabrics onto the calico. Attach hoop to your bear's hand using a strong thread. ❈

ARMS

Attach the paws to the arms pieces, matching the dots. Stitch the white hands together with the white thread, then join inner and outer arms, leaving a gap at the back where marked.

JOINTING

Place a washer, then a disc onto a bolt and place inside the head, with the bolt protruding out the hole, left in the neck. Insert bolt into the neck opening in the body and attach another disc, then a washer onto the bolt inside the body. Attach a locknut and tighten using a spanner and screwdriver.

Attach limbs to the body in the same way, making first marking a hole at the joint marks with an awl. Place a washer, then a poselimp eyelet and disc onto the bolt to be placed inside the limbs. Complete the joint as for the head.

Note: For firm joints, tighten until you can't move the limbs, then loosen one-half turn. The denser the fabric pile, the more the limbs will loosen over time.

STUFFING

Stuff the head very firmly using small amounts of stuffing at a time. Start in the nose area, making this very firm so that you can embroider the nose neatly. Close the opening with a Ladder Stitch. Stuff the body firmly with stuffing, especially around the joints. A stuffing tool or chopstick can be used. Fill the limbs halfway with the coarse river sand, then fill the rest of the way with stuffing. Close the opening with Ladder Stitch.

GLASS EYES

Using an awl, make a small hole at each eye position. With very strong thread and the long doll needle, take needle through the centre base of the neck at the back of the head to the eye position.

Loop through the eye, then insert needle back into the same hole and across to the other eye position. Loop through the eye, then take the needle back through the same hole to the back of the head, about 5mm from the entry point.

Press the eyes firmly into the head, forming eye sockets and gives the bear more character. Knot the ends of the thread securely, then re-thread the ends into the needle and draw ends into the head, exit at another point, pull tightly and cut off. The ends will then sink back into the head.

NOSE

Clip the fur pile very close in the shape and position of the nose. Cut out a suede or felt template in the shape you require and glue into position. Pin the smile into position, centring over the throat seam, about 1.5cm down from the base of the nose. Embroider over the nose template with even, firm pressure on the threads, following the guide on the pattern sheet. Embroider the mouth, taking stitches form A to C, then on to B and back to C.

Anchor with the small vertical stitches show at A and B. Take the thread from C back to the centre, base of the nose and finish off by taking the thread back and forth beneath the nose a couple of times, then out the base of the head. Pull firmly and cut threads. ❁

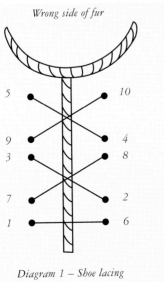

Wrong side of fur

Diagram 1 – Shoe lacing

Mrs Stitchem

Mrs Stitchem, made by Anne Riesborough, carries her sewing kit with her at all times, ready to fly into action with her needle and thread. Most of the materials used in this project you will find in your fabric scrap box.

PREPARATION

Trace the patterns onto tracing paper, transferring all markings. The pattern includes a 5mm (¼in) seam allowance. Trace pattern onto fabric, reversing pieces where indicated. Cut out fur with small, pointed scissors, cutting the backing fabric and not the fur pile.

SEWING AND STUFFING

Stitch the head pieces from tip of the nose to base of neck. Baste the head gusset between the side head pieces, matching the notch on the gusset to the front seam, and easing to fit. Sew, clip curves and turn out. Stuff the head firmly with the polyester stuffing, then run a gathering thread around neck using the strong thread. Assemble joint and inset into the head with pin protruding from the neck. Draw up the gathering thread tightly around joint and tie off securely.

Stitch body pieces together, leaving an opening as indicated on the pattern. Using an awl, ease a small hole in the top of the body for the neck joint. Insert split pin from the head and attach the washer, then turn down the ends of he pin so the head is secured firmly. Stitch arms, leaving an opening as indicated on the pattern. Attach joints to the inside of arms as for the head, or stuff firmly then attach them with button thread, sewing from one arm through the body to the other arm, several times.

Stuff the body with a thin layer of stuffing, then spoon glass pellets into the body until it feels well-weighted. Finish filling the body with stuffing and ladder-stitch the opening closed. Attach eyes on seam where marked, using strong thread. Insert the needle from the base of the neck at the back of head. Direct needle to the eye position, thread eye, then insert needle back into the same hole and through to the other eye. Insert needle again and bring out at the back of the head where you stated. Pull threads tightly and tie off. Stitch around the curved edge of the ears and tun out. Fold in the raw edges at the base and ladder-stitch ears to Mrs Stitchem's head.

CLOTHING

Dress: Cut out pattern pieces for dress, plus a skirt piece 31cm x 10cm, from the print fabric. Cut out apron pattern from the contrast fabric, with a pocket piece 5cm square for the thimble. Cut out the lining in one piece and the pincushion from the flannel.

Sew front and back bodice pieces together at the shoulders. Turn under the neck edge 3mm and top-stitch. Gather the tops of the sleeves to fit armholes and stitch. Turn sleeve edges under and top-stitch. Top-stitch lace on seamline around armhole to make a pretty shoulder frill and do the same around the sleeve hems. Sew sleeve and bodice side seams.

Gather top of skirt to fit bodice and stitch with right sides together.

Turn up the hem twice to hide raw edges and stitch. You can fit this to your bear. Press under the back seam allowance from the neck edge to the hem, place dress on bear and hand-sew the back of the dress closed with a ladder stitch.

Apron: Cut out one apron piece and one bib piece from the contrast fabric, with a pocket piece 5cm square for the thimble. Cut the hat from the same fabric. Cut out complete apron piece for the lining from flannel. Cut a circle the same as the hat from flannel for the pincushion.

Turn down the top seam allowance on the lower apron piece and top-stitch lace to edge. Tack lower apron over the

FINISHED SIZE:

• 13cm (5¼in)

MATERIALS:

• 45cm x 23cm (18in x 9in) mohair with a map no longer than 5mm (¼in)

• Small amount of fabric for dress

• Small amount of fabric for apron and mob hat.

• Small piece of flannel for pin cushion and apron lining

• 50cm (½yd) lace of your choice

• 1m (1yd) ribbon for apron straps and decoration

• 6mm (¼in) eyes

• 20cm x 15mm (8in x ⅝in) elastic

• Set of small washers and split pins for joints

• Glass pellets to give weight to the bear.

• Brown embroidery thread for nose

• Polyester stuffing

• Round spring tape measure

• Scissors, thimble, quick unpick and pins to decorate

• General sewing requirements

base of the bib piece. Stitch around outside edge of apron and lining with right sides together. Turn out through the pocket and press.

Top-stitch from the top of the pocket to the hem, dividing the pocket in two. Turn down the top edge of the thimble pocket pieces and top-stitch lace across the tip. Turn under the remaining seam allowance and press, then stitch to the front of apron. Top-stitch lace around the remaining edges of the apron and attach ribbon ties to the bib and sides of the apron. Stitch two small bows to the top of the bib and top of the thimble pocket.

Neaten the edge of the hat piece with a zigzag stitch or overlocker and top-

stitch lace around edge, joining ends of lace with a zigzag stitch. Run a gathering stitch around the outside edge of pincushion and stuff firmly with stuffing. Pull in gathering threads and tie off. Tack pincushion to bear's head, cover with the hat and tie with ribbon, making a bow at the front.

Stitch elastic to the base of the bear, crossing over to form a casing for the tape measure. Place the spring mechanism for the tape measure at the top so when you press down on the bear, the tape springs back. Mrs Stitchem carries scissors and an unpicker in her bib pockets, and a thimble in her lower pocket. Her hat is always full of pins.

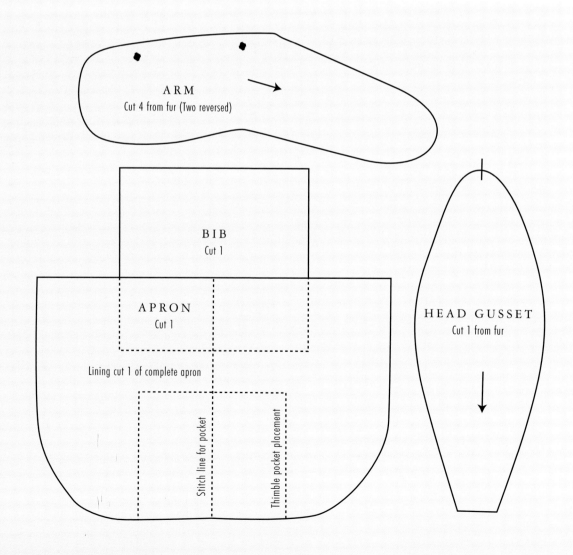

ARM
Cut 4 from fur (Two reversed)

BIB
Cut 1

APRON
Cut 1

Lining cut 1 of complete apron

Stitch line for pocket

Thimble pocket placement

HEAD GUSSET
Cut 1 from fur

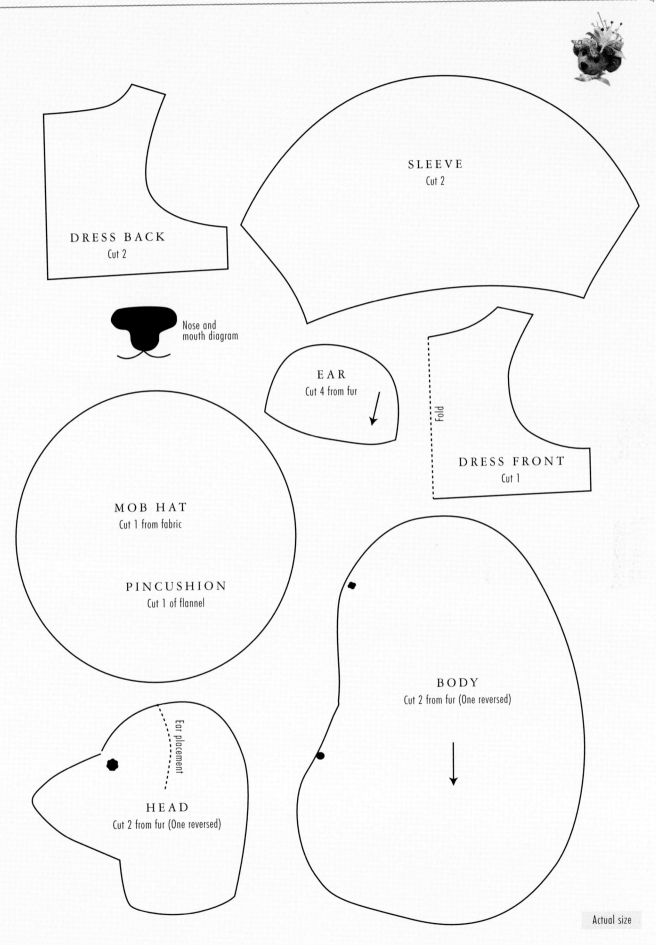

DRESS BACK
Cut 2

SLEEVE
Cut 2

Nose and
mouth diagram

EAR
Cut 4 from fur

Fold

DRESS FRONT
Cut 1

MOB HAT
Cut 1 from fabric

PINCUSHION
Cut 1 of flannel

BODY
Cut 2 from fur (One reversed)

Ear placement

HEAD
Cut 2 from fur (One reversed)

Actual size

Daniel

Daniel is a very special bear, made by Lexi Haworth, dedicated to the memory of the grandson of a dear friend. Made from short mohair and dressed in his fiery red tracksuit, Daniel is simply charming.

PREPARATION

Copy the pattern and paste onto cardboard. Position pieces according the fabric pile and trace onto backing fabric, transferring all markings. Check that pieces are correct before cutting the fabric. Cut fabric with small snips and avoid cutting the fur pile. Cut the paw pads form the leather. A 5mm seam allowance is included in the pattern. Seams should be pinned and tacked with a wide overcast stitch, then either machined or backstitched.

HEAD

Place the side head pieces right sides together and stitch the centre front seam from A to B under the chin. Pin and stitch the head gusset in position, matching the centre notch to the seam at A, leaving an opening where marked. Using the dental floss, run a gathering thread around the neck and draw up tightly, leaving just enough space for he head screw to pass through. Turn right side out.

ARMS

Stitch the paw pads to the inside arm pieces. Pin the inside and outside arm pieces right sides together and stitch, leaving an opening as indicated.

LEGS

Stitch legs, with right sides together, leaving an opening as indicated on the pattern. Pin the foot pad in place, matching the notch on the pad inplace, matching the notch on the pad to the centre front seam. Stitch, easing the pad around evenly as you go. This may be easier to stitch by hand, especially on small bears.

BODY

Sew the darts at the top and base of the body pieces, then pin pieces right sides together and stitch, matching darts. Leave an opening at the back as indicated on the pattern (for stuffing) and a small opening at the top dart for the head screw. Turn right side out.

EARS

Stitch around the curved edge, then turn right side out. Turn under the raw edges 5mm at the base and overcast together with dental floss. Pull firmly as you stitch to cup the ear. Leave a length of thread to attach the ear to the head.

ASSEMBLING YOUR BEAR

Head: Place a washer, then a 35mm disc onto a screw and place the assembly into the head through the top opening with the shaft protruding through the hole left in the neck. Place the end of the screw into the hole at the top of the body. Place another disc, then a metal washer and locknut onto the screw inside the body and finger-tighten.

Continue to tighten using a ring spanner while turning the head of the screw with a screwdriver.

MATERIALS:

- 50cm (20in) square short, sparse mohair or acrylic
- 15cm(6in) square soft leather for paw pads
- Black glass eyes
- 8 x 30mm (1¼in) discs for arms and legs
- 2x 35mm (1½in) discs for head
- 5 screws with locknuts and 10 washers
- Black perle thread for nose and claws
- Matching sewing thread
- Waxed dental floss
- Polyester stuffing, about 250g (9oz)
- Plastic pellets, about 200g (7oz)
- An old nylon stocking (optional)
- Fine-tip pen
- Small, sharp pointed scissors
- Doll needle
- Stuffing stick
- Small long-nose pliers
- Ring spanner to fit locknuts
- Small screwdriver
- General sewing requirements

Stuff head firmly with small amounts of stuffing at a time. Pay particular attention to the nose area which should be very firm, and mould the shape of the head as you go. Close the opening with a Ladder Stitch using dental floss. Pin the ears into position and ladder-stitch to the head with the length of dental floss left attached to the ears.

EYES

❖

Attach the eyes at this stage. Using our bear as a guide, make a small hole in each eye position. Thread a double length of dental floss through the loop at the back of the eye, then thread the ends onto a long needle. Push the needle into the head through the eye hole and out at the base of the head. Use the pliers to pull the needle through if you find it difficult. Repeat this procedure for the other eye, bringing the threads out close together. Pull tightly on both sets of threads to make the eyes sink into the head and create sockets. This gives the bear a more natural expression. Tie in a reef knot and thread the ends back into the head.

ARMS AND LEGS

Make holes in the inner arms and legs and on the body with pointed scissors at the joint marks. Assemble and attach joints as for the head. Pellets have been used in Daniel's arms, legs and tummy to achieve a nice floppy feel and to help him sit nicely. Begin by stuffing his paws and feet very firmly. This is especially important when using leather for the paw pads. Stuff the tops of the arms and legs firmly around the discs, then pour pellets into the centre. Move the limb around a little to disperse the pellets evenly. Cover the opening with a little stuffing and ladder-stitch the opening closed using dental floss.

BODY

Stuff the body firmly around the neck area and around the arm and leg joints. Place a small amount of stuffing in the lower part of the tummy, then pour in the pellets. The pellets can be replaced inside the toe area of an old stocking, but make sure they have room to move around freely. Cover the opening with some stuffing, then close with a Ladder Stitch using dental floss.

NOSE

Carefully embroider the nose with the Perlé thread and the doll needle, again using our bear as a guide. Use a Satin Stitch with even stitches and don't pull too tightly. Begin at the centre of the nose, working out to the sides, reducing the size of the stitches as you go. A few stitches in the centre extend down to the lip. Repeat for the other side. The mouth is stitched using single straight stitches. If you don't get it right the first time, just pull out the threads carefully with the long-nose pliers and start again. ✼

Simply Huggable

Tinderbox Bears

These adorable posable bears are made by Jedda Sorensen
and are ideal to have sitting around the house.
They may take some time to make but are very easy to construct.

PREPARATION

❖

Read instructions before proceding. Trace patterns for clothing and body from the pattern sheet, transferring all markings. A 5mm (¼in) seam allowance is included.

MODELLING THE CLAY

❖

Head: Start by getting a ball of clay about the size of a 20c piece. Knead this until it is soft, then roll it into a rounded cone shape. Using your thumb, make an indentation half way down the cone for the eye placement. The pointed half is the nose and the larger half is the top of the head. Make a hole in the bottom of the head with a skewer where the pipe cleaner body will be attached. It will be easier if you leave the skewer in the head and hold this when adding the other features. Experiment with the shape until you are pleased with it.

Ears: Roll two small balls of clay, half the size of a pea, then flatten out and pinch together one end. Score the head for the desired placement of the ears, then press on the ears using a large needle or something similar.

Eyes: Roll up two tiny balls of clay and place in the desired position.

Nose: Roll up another piece of clay into an oval shape and press onto the pointed end to form a nose.

Hands: Using a ball of clay the size of a 5c piece, roll into a slightly flattened cylinder and curve one end to create the hand. At the other end, make a hole with a knitting needle for the placement of the pipe-cleaner arm. Repeat this step for the other hand.

Feet: Roll a ball of clay into a cylinder as before, then bend into a right angle halfway down. Flatten one half into the foot and at the other end make a hole. Repeat for other foot.

Create a texture in the clay by pressing various objects into the clay after it has been modelled, as it is then easier to paint.

Polymer clays are baked in a conventional oven and the time depends on the brand of clay. See packet for baking instructions.

PAINTING

❖

For an opaque finish, simply paint twice with acrylic paint. Finish with acrylic varnish. For a more transparent finish, thin down the acrylic paint to a watercolour consistency. If using Modelene, the body pieces may need to be washed in water and dried so the paint adheres correctly.

Using the No. 3 paint brush, apply the first coat in a darker colour, for example Jo Sonja's Burnt Umber, so it will show under the other coats. Proceed with another two or three coats of the second lighter colour, for example, Burnt Sienna. Make sure you use a soft brush so fewer streaks appear.

Using the No 00 brush, paint the nose and eyes black. Leave the pieces for several hours to ensure they are dry. Finish by applying a coat or two of Acrylic Satin Varnish over all pieces, using a soft No 3 or 4 brush.

Note: To make it easier to paint, place each body piece on a matchstick.

THE BODY FRAME

❖

Cut a pipe-cleaner into two lengths, one piece 17cm (6¾in) and the other 10.5cm (4¼in). Fold the longer pipe-cleaner in a

FINISHED SIZE:

- 10cm (4in)

MATERIALS:

- 50g polymer clay (Artist's Modelene has been used here)
- Acrylic paints in two shades of brown and black
- Acrylic satin varnish
- Good quality watercolour paint brushes in sizes 00, 3, 4
- Packet white pipe-cleaners
- 25cm (10in) calico
- Matching sewing thread
- Glue gun or fast drying glue
- Scraps of material for clothing
- Polyester stuffing
- Large sewing needle or knitting needle
- Long-nosed pliers
- Skewer
- General sewing requirements

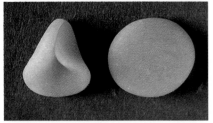

half twist a quarter of the way down to create a body and legs. See diagram. Crimp top with pliers to ensure it is small enough to fit into the hole in the head. Twist the other pipe-cleaner around body near the top for the arms. Crimp to secure.

Place a bead of glue on the end of each pip-cleaner and insert into corresponding body piece.

Create a hem in the calico at the arms and legs by folding the fabric under, adjusting the length to fit the limbs. Stitch around the end of the calico and draw it in so it is covering the top of the limb, making sure the pipe-cleaner cannot be seen.

The calico can also be glued into place if desired. Stitch around the opening at the neck and draw it in.

THE CALICO BODY

Cut out body and sew with a 5mm (¼in) seam allowance, leaving ankles, wrists and head open. Clip under arms and crotch, then turn right side out. Insert the pipe-cleaner body into the calico, feet first. Add stuffing, mostly around the middle. Trim pipe-cleaner if you want shorter limbs. Do not rim the calico body, as any excess can be folded under and it is better to have extra fabric than not enough.

ADDING BODY PIECES

Trim off some of the fluff around the end of the pip-cleaners where they are going to be instead into the limbs and head.

CLOTHING

Dress: Hem back pieces at the centre back opening, ensuring there is enough fabric overlapping to secure a tiny button. Place the front and back pieces right sides together and stitch shoulder seams. Hem the armholes. Stitch the side seams and hem the bottom of the dress. Hand sew the neck edge to neaten. Turn right side out and add little pieces of lace and buttons if desired.

Top: Make the top in the same way as the dress.

Trousers: Hem the waist and leg of each trouser piece using 5mm (¼in) seam allowance. With right sides together, stitch inside leg seams, match up seams and stitch crotch seam. The little bear's trouser are kept up with a piece of string or leather tied around the waist. ❈

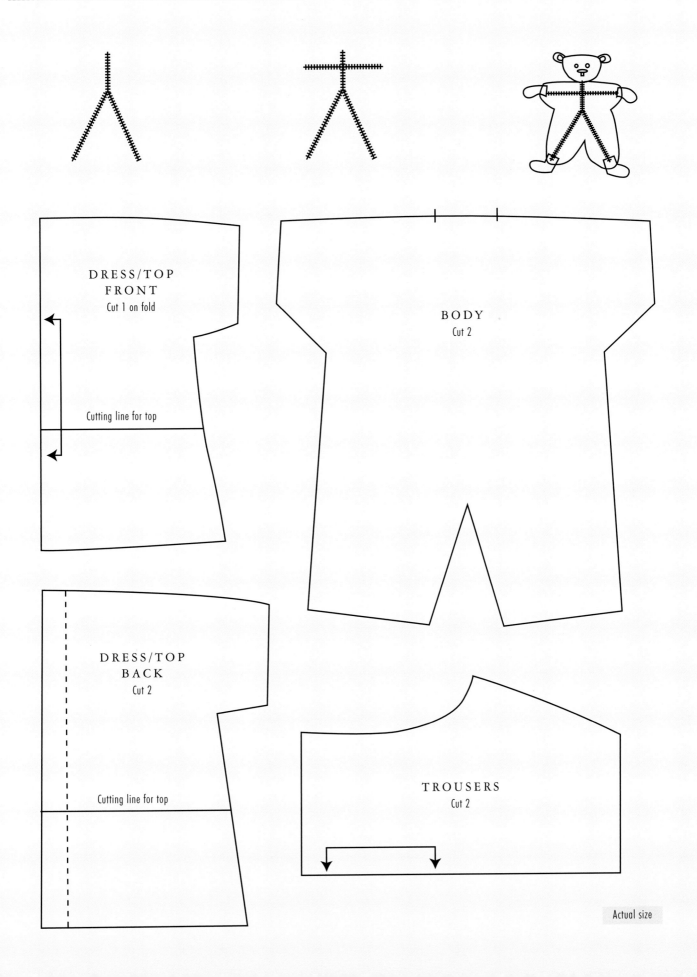

DRESS/TOP
FRONT
Cut 1 on fold

Cutting line for top

DRESS/TOP
BACK
Cut 2

Cutting line for top

BODY
Cut 2

TROUSERS
Cut 2

Actual size

Angelica

This angelic creature will surely lift your spirits when you're feeling blue. Designed by Adele Rowe, Angelica happily sways along to the tune on her music box.

PREPARATION

Read instructions carefully before commencing your bear. A 4mm seam allowance is included in the pattern. Trace the pattern pieces onto template plastic and cut out. Mark the reverse (wrong side) of the fabric with an arrow to indicate the direction of the fur pile. Place pattern pieces onto the fabric with the arrows following the lay of the fur pile. Trace around each pattern piece, reversing relevant pieces where indicated and marking all openings, eye, arm and leg joint positions. Cut out all pieces using sharp embroidery scissors, ensuring you cut only the backing fabric and not the fur pile. Trace and cut out paw and foot pad pieces from leather, suede, felt or other selected material.

SEWING

Note: All pieces should be pinned at right angles to the cut edge, overcast with polyester thread and then machine or hand-stitched.

HEAD

After cutting out the pattern pieces, trim back fur to the exact 4mm seam allowance on both the side-head pieces and the head gusset.

With right sides together, pin and sew the side-head pieces together from the nose, under the chin, and down to the neck. Pin and sew the head gusset to the side-head pieces, matching the centre front seam of the gusset to the nose position on the side-head pieces. Turn the head right side out.

BODY

Sew the darts at the base of each body piece. With right sides facing, pin and sew the body pieces together, leaving the openings as marked on the pattern pieces.

ARMS

Match the paw pad to the inner arm and sew in place. With right sides together, sew the outer arm to the inner arm, leaving an opening for stuffing as indicated on the pattern. Turn right side out. Repeat for the other arm.

LEGS

With right sides together, pin and sew the inner leg to the outer leg, leaving openings as marked on the pattern pieces. Pin the centre front of the foot pad to the toe of the leg and the centre back of the foot pad to the heel of the leg. Sew around the entire foot pad. Turn right side out. Repeat for the other leg.

JOINTING

Arms and legs: If using the waggle-shaft music box it is recommended that locknut jointing (with a short screw) be used due to the size of the music box. Using your awl, make joint holes where indicated on the pattern pieces. For each joint, place a washer, then a disc onto a bolt into the joint holes marked on the inner arms and inner leg pieces. Push the

MATERIALS

- Fat eighth of English mohair (a fat quarter cut in half)

- 15cm (6in) square of leather, suede, felt or other fabric for paw/foot pad

- 9mm ($^5/_8$in) glass eyes

- 4 x 30mm (1$^1/_8$in) wooden discs for arms

- 4 x 35mm (1$^3/_8$in) wooden discs for legs

- 4 x 16mm ($^5/_8$in) setscrews, 4 locknits and 8 washers

- Music box and waggle shaft

- Angel wings

- Gold paint for wings

- 1m (1$^1/_8$yd) wired gold organdy ribbon for bow

- Light brown silk embroidery thread and gold thread

- Polyester stuffing

- Doll needle

- Awl

- Screwdriver and spanner for locknuts

- Stuffing stick

- Sharp embroidery scissors

- Template plastic

- Polyester thread to match back of fabric

- Fray-stopping liquid (optional)

- General sewing requirements

FINISHED SIZE:

28cm (11in)

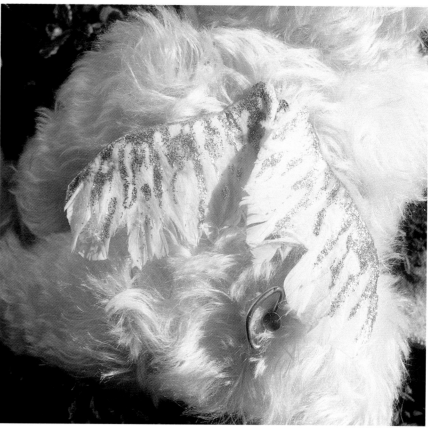

bolt through the joint positions marked on the body and secure with another disc, washer and locknut. Tighten the locknut using a screwdriver and spanner.

STUFFING AND FINISHING

Arms and legs: Stuff the arms and legs firmly, making sure the filling is pushed well down into the paws and around the ankle areas. Close all openings using a fine Ladder Stitch.

Head: Stuff the head, moulding it into shape as you go and ensuring the nose and crown area are firmly stuffed. Loosely stuff the neck area of the head to enable the waggle shaft to move freely once inserted. Using a stuffing tool or chopstick, make a channel through the stuffing for the top of the waggle shaft. Fill part of the body, then insert the music box, pushing the waggle shaft up through the opening at the top of the body. Finish stuffing the body, making sure the filling is quite loose at the top to enable maximum movement of the waggle shaft. Place the head over the top of the waggle shaft, fold in fur as marked on the pattern, and matching chin seam to centre front seam and middle of gusset at rear to centre back seam, ladder-stitch the head to the top of the body with extra strong thread. Close the opening at the back of the body with Ladder Stitch.

EARS

With right sides facing, pin and sew matching ear pieces together. trim the corners and turn right side out. Close openings with a small slip stitch. Pin the ears to the head in the desired position and sew firmly into place.

FINISHING

Mark desired eye positions with a pin. make a hole in the desired position with your awl or knitting needle. thread a needle with doubled strong cotton thread through the loop of the glass eye. Thread the ends onto a long doll needle and insert the needle into the eye hole and bring it out at the back of the head. Sink the eye by pulling firmly on the thread and secure with a knot. Bury the threads into the head. Repeat for the other eye.

Embroider nose and mouth using light brown silk thread. Angelica's nose was created using a light brown silk thread overstitched with gold thread. Embellish the angel wings with gold glitter paint and sew to the back of the bear. make a bow using a gold organdy ribbon with wired edges and secure to Angelica's head.❖

Gilly

Gilly is a charming country bear who clearly wears her heart for all to see. Denise Matthews of Denise and Friends has designed this well-loved bear, complete with worn paw pads and sparse mohair.

PREPARATION

Read all of the instructions carefully before commencing your bear. A 3mm (1/8in) seam allowance is included in the pattern pieces. Trace all pattern pieces onto cardboard or templastic to retain an original copy of the pattern.

Mark the wrong side of your fabric with an arrow to denote the fur pile direction. Place pattern pieces onto the fabric, matching the arrows with the fur pile direction. Trace around each pattern piece with a fabric marking pen, reversing the pieces where indicated and marking all openings and joint positions. Cut out the pattern using small sharp scissors, taking care to cut only the backing fabric and not the fur pile. Cut the foot pads from the leather or suede.

SEWING

Trim the fur around the head gusset and the side head pieces where indicated on the pattern pieces. Stitch the darts on each of the side head pieces. With right sides together, pin and sew the head pieces together from the tip of the nose, down the chin to the base of the neck. Pin the head gusset to the side head pieces and sew from the nose, around the top of the head, to the back of the neck. Repeat for the other side. Turn right side out.

EARS

Match ears in pairs and with right sides together, pin and sew around the curve, leaving the straight edge open. Turn right side out. Tuck the raw edge under and overstitch together. Repeat for the other ear.

BODY

Sew darts on both body pieces. With right sides facing, pin and sew the body pieces together, leaving an opening where indicated on the pattern. Make holes for the joint marks with an awl or knitting needle. Turn right side out.

ARMS

Match the paw pad with the edge of the inner arm and, with right sides together, pin and sew in place. (if you are using leather, do not pin the paw pads as the pins leave marks.) Fold the arm in half with right sides together and sew around the arm, leaving an opening where indicated on the pattern. Make joint holes, where marked, with your awl, making sure the hole is on the inner arm. Turn right side out. Repeat for the other arm.

LEGS

Fold one leg piece in half and with right sides together, pin and sew from the toe, up around the top of the leg, leaving an opening where indicated and at the base of the foot. Sew the foot pad to the base of the foot, easing it in place and ensuring the notches line up at the front and back. Make a joint hole with your awl or knitting needle. Turn right side out. Repeat these steps for the other leg.

FINISHED SIZE:

- 31cm (12in)

MATERIALS

- 73cm x 50cm (29in x 20in)sparse mohair
- 23cm x 12cm (9in x 5in) leather or suede for paw pads
- 8mm (3/8in) glass eyes
- Joints: 8 x 2.5cm (1in) hardwood discs, 2 x 3.75cm (1½in) hardwood discs with cotter-pin holes, 4 x locknuts and bolts, 8 washers, 1 x 36mm (1½in) cotter pin and 2 small washers
- Polyester stuffing
- Plastic pellets
- Fabric-marking pen
- Matching thread
- Strong thread or dental floss
- Small, sharp scissors
- Awl or knitting needle
- Long doll needle
- Pointed-nose pliers or cotter-pin turner
- Phillip's head screwdriver and spanner
- Stuffing tool
- Black or brown Perlé Cotton
- Glass pins
- Toothpick or crochet hook
- Brush
- Sandpaper
- Cardboard or templastic
- General sewing requirements

ASSEMBLY

Using small amounts of polyester stuffing and a stuffing tool, fill your bear's head very firmly, beginning at the nose. Fill the rest of the head with polyester stuffing, making sure it is stuffed evenly. Assemble the cotter-pin joint and place it into the base of the head. Using strong thread or dental floss, run a gathering stitch around the base of the neck. Draw the thread up tightly around the head of the cotter pin and tie off securely. Make a small hole in the top of the body and insert the protruding cotter pin. Then place a disc and washer on the cotter pin shaft. Using pliers or a cotter-pin tool, curl the cotter pin as tightly as possible to secure. Check that the centre seams on the head and the body are aligned.

ARMS AND LEGS

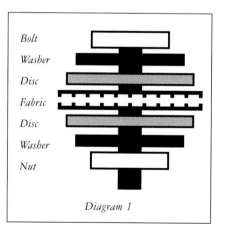

Diagram 1

Place a washer and disc onto a bolt and insert through the joint markings. Insert the protruding bolts into the body joint marks where indicated and secure with a disc, washer and locknut (diagram 1). Tighten securely using a spanner and Phillips head screwdriver. Stuff the limbs firmly with polyester stuffing, ensuring they are even. Ladder-stitch to close.

BODY

Fill the bottom part of the body with polyester stuffing. Continue to fill the body with pellets until you achieve the desired effect. To finish, add wads of polyester stuffing around the shoulders and the hump at the back. Ladder-stitch to close.

FINISHING

Experiment with ear placement and use a pin to mark their intended position. The ears will be sewn in place at a later stage.

ATTACHING THE EARS

Position the ears where marked previously, ensuring they cover the small stitches created by the eye placement. ladder-stitch the ears in place.

EYES

Use glass pins and experiment with eye placement. When satisfied with their location, make eye holes with your awl or knitting needle. Thread a long doll needle with doubled thread. Knot the ends securely. Insert the needle through the eye hole and exit at the pin that marks the ear position. Take a stitch and thread the needle back through the head and exit at the first eye position. Thread the needle through the shank of the eye and enter into the head, exiting at the other socket. Thread the second eye onto the needle into the head, exiting at

the ear mark on the same side. Pull up tightly and tie off securely.

NOSE

Embroider the nose and mouth using Perlé Cotton. Embroider three claws on each of the paws and feet. Use a toothpick or crochet hook to pull out any fur that has been caught in the seams and give the bear a good brush. Sandpaper the leather paw and foot pads for a worn look.❉

Cittie and Ema

Susan Milsom has designed this endearing little bear made in curly-style mohair. Cittie has her own little toy bear Ema to keep her company.

PREPARATION

❖

Read all instructions carefully. Transfer pattern from the pattern sheet, making sure to mark all joints and openings. following the pattern layout, place pattern pieces onto the fabric, with arrows following he direction of the fur and the pieces reversed where indicated. After laying out all pieces, trace lightly around outside of each piece with the felt-tip pen. Using small sharp scissors, carefully cut out, making sure not to cut the pile. Cut paw and footpads from velour fabric. Before starting to sew, pin all pieces together, taking care to tuck in fur away from the seams.

STITCHING

❖

If hand-sewing, use a back or overcast stitch, ensuring all stitching is firm. If machine-sewing, leaving a 3mm seam allowance. Where paw and feet fabric meet fur, tack and backstitch by hand.

STARTING YOUR BEAR

❖

Head: Stitch side head pieces from nose to neck. Pin in head gusset, sewing from nose to neck on each side. Cut slits in heads for ears where marked.

Ears: Sew ear pieces together, leaving open along base where marked. Turn the ears right side out. Slip one ear at a time in to the slits on head, tack into place, then sew across.

Eyes: Make small holes where marked on the head. Turn head right side out and insert eyes into the holes. Visually check eyes are even. Secure eyes on the inside of the head by pressing the flange down hard on the eye shaft, right to the fabric.

Body: Stitch around body, leaving opening in back as marked. Make hole for joints as marked, then turn body right side out.

Arms: Stitch paw pad to each inside arm. Make sure the curve of the paw matches the outside arm pieces. Stitch inner and outer arm pieces together, leaving opening where marked. Make hole for joint and turn right side out.

Legs: Fold legs in half and sew together, leaving opening as marked. Match leg to correct foot pad, and sew around the outside. Turn the leg right side out.

JOINTING

❖

Thread a washer and a wooden disc onto a bolt and insert into an arm with the bolt extending through the hole. Place bolt through corresponding hole in the body and attach wooden disc, washer and locknut inside the body. Tighten the joint firmly with a spanner, then repeat the process with other arm and legs.

Note: Locknut joints are preferred as they result in a good firm joint, however, plastic joints may be substituted if you are not confident with using the wooden joints.

STUFFING

❖

Head: Starting with the nose, using small amounts of fill at a time, stuff head firmly. Using a large stitch, draw the base of the neck together, as this will be sewn to body later.

Arms: Start with a small amount of fill to stuff the paws, using the stuffing tool. Build up from the foot right through to the top of the leg, making sure the fill is

MATERIALS FOR CITTIE:

- 50cm x 54cm (^{1}/2yd x 21^1/2in) curly style mohair fur fabric
- 15cm x 14cm (6in x 5^1/2in) velour paw pad fabric
- 8cm x 5mm (3^1/4in x 1^3/4in) wooden discs
- 4 x ^{3}/16in machine bolts
- 4 x nylon locknuts and machine washers
- Black embroidery cotton for nose
- Brown embroidery cotton for had
- Black 12mm (^{1}/2in) safety eyes
- Cotton filing for stuffing
- 200g (^{1}/2lb) plastic pellets
- 45cm (18in) tea-dyed cotton bow
- 25cm (^{1}/4yd) plastic pearl string
- Sewing cotton to match fabric
- Small sharp scissors
- Spanner
- Fine black felt-tip pen
- General sewing requirements

MATERIALS FOR EMA:

- 28cm x 24cm (^{3}/8 yd x 9^1/2in) tea-dyed calico
- Small wooden button
- 25cm (^{1}/2yd) twine
- Black embroidery cotton

tightly packed around each joint. Use a Ladder Stitch to close the openings

Legs: Start by stuffing the foot tightly using the stuffing tool. Build up from the foot right through to the top of the leg, making sure fill is tightly packed around each joint. Stitch opening closed with a ladder stitch.

Body: Arms and legs should already be attached and stuffed. Use the plastic beads to fill first third of tummy, then complete stuffing body with cotton fill (beads are optional). Place cotton fill around the hump and top of body quite firmly so the head will sit correctly when attached. Ladder-stitch closed.

SEWING ON HEAD

Place head on a slight tilt to the left. Using an embroidery needle and thread, tack front and back of neck to body. When in place, sew from front, right around the neck to the front again, then around once more.

NOSE AND MOUTH

Trim back the fur from the nose to eyes, and also around and under chin. This defines muzzle clearly. Using black embroidery cotton, stitch the outline of nose, then fill in with Satin Stitch. Use straight stitches to form the mouth into a big smile.

MAKING EMA

Cut two body pieces from calico fabric and stitch the two halves together, leaving an opening where marked, then stuff firmly with cotton fill.

Use the stuffing tool to get the stuffing into small areas, then close the opening with Ladder Stitch. Sew on button with black embroidery cotton. Mark eyes and mouth on toy with black felt-tip pen. ❁

EMA
Cut 2

Leave open

133%

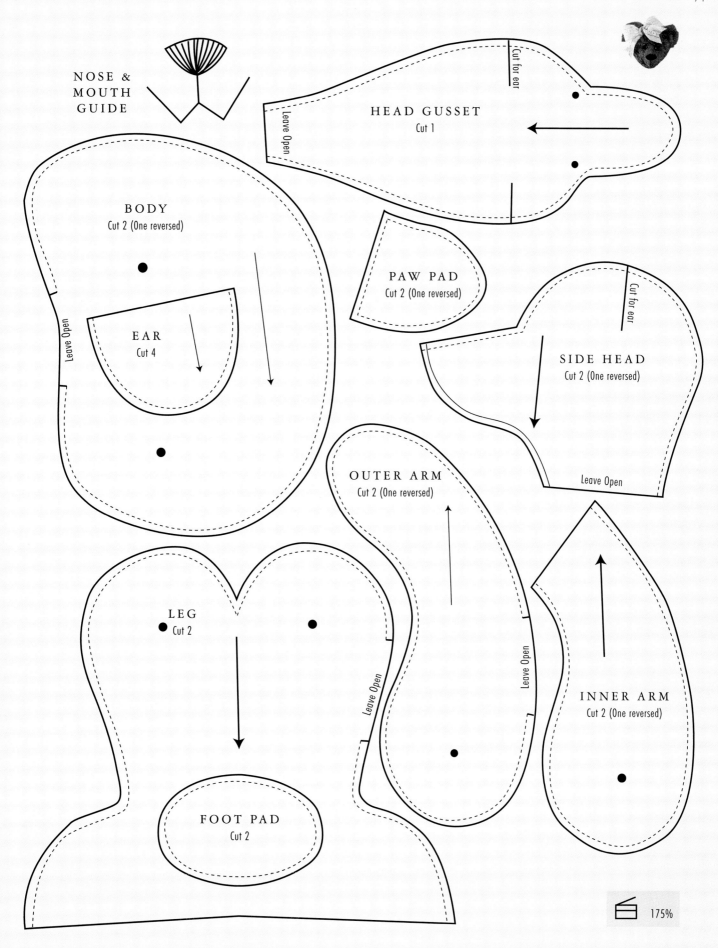

NOSE &
MOUTH
GUIDE

HEAD GUSSET
Cut 1

Leave Open

Cut for ear

BODY
Cut 2 (One reversed)

Leave Open

EAR
Cut 4

PAW PAD
Cut 2 (One reversed)

SIDE HEAD
Cut 2 (One reversed)

Cut for ear

Leave Open

OUTER ARM
Cut 2 (One reversed)

Leave Open

Leave Open

INNER ARM
Cut 2 (One reversed)

LEG
Cut 2

FOOT PAD
Cut 2

175%

Beary Special!

Georgia

Gorgeous Georgia looks as good as gold in her school uniform, but beware of her mischievous streak! Designed by Mariette Noorman from Mariette's Bears, at 50cm (20in) Georgia is big enough to stand on her own two feet.

PREPARATION

Allow a 4mm (³/₁₆in) seam allowance around all pattern pieces. Carefully trace the pattern onto the quilter's template plastic, transferring all markings. Trace the pattern onto the back of fabric, taking care to note the direction of the pile and arrows on the pattern pieces. Using small, sharp scissors, cut the fur pile. Paw pads may be cut out from mohair, felt or suede.

STITCHING

Stitching can be done by hand or by machine. Always pin pieces with the right sides together, then stitch. When hand-sewing, overcast seams, going back over them with a small Backstitch using doubled thread. Use a single thread for overcasting.

Arms: Stitch paw pads to inner arm. Pin inner and outer arms together and sew. Leave openings as shown.

Legs: Stitch legs right sides together. Leave an opening at back. Snip in corner notches around the ankle, being careful not to cut the seam stitching. Pin on the foot pads, matching markings to seams and overcast edges. You may find it easier to do this by hand – sewing with a small backstitch.

Body: Sew in darts at the bottom. Pin pieces right sides together and sew, carefully matching the darts. Leave an opening in the back and a small at the marking for the head. Using the awl, pierce a hole where marked on inner arms, legs and body. Turn all pieces right side out. Stuff feet and paws using small pieces of polyester filling.

Head: Join Georgia's head at nose (A) to neck (B). With right sides together, pin these pieces and overcast the edges, pushing the fur pile inwards as you stitch.

Pin and stitch the head gusset into position, matching centre (C) to seam at (A). Ease the gusset if necessary. Turn right side out.

Ears: Stitch curved edges of the ears together. Turn to right sides. Turn in raw edges and using a long piece of dental floss, hand-sew across the base of the ear, leaving the thread hanging. Take time to find the correct position for Georgia's ears. Place approx 1cm inside the gusset. When satisfied, sew in place with the threads that were left hanging, using Ladder Stitch. Finish of securely.

JOINTING

Using only small pieces of stuffing, especially at the nose, stuff the head firmly, stopping occasionally to mould Georgia's face into shape with your hands. When satisfied, use doubled dental floss to run a gathering stitch around the neck, taking care not to pull too tightly.

Assembling neck joint: Place a small washer over a 35mm cotter pin. Put a 35mm disc onto the cotter pin, placing it in the neck opening with the pin facing outwards. Draw the gathering threads as firmly as possible around the pin and finish off securely. The cotter pin should now be protruding from the head.

Attaching head: The cotter pin is passed through the small opening left in the neck on the body. Place the wooden disc and a washer over the cotter pin and roll down the sides very firmly onto the washer using the pliers.

Arms and legs: Make holes at the joint marks using an awl. Insert the bolt through both washer and disc and from inside the arm at the joint and mark to the outside. Push the bolt through the body where marked and secure it using a socket spanner. Make sure all the joints are very

FINISHED SIZE:

Approx 50cm (20in)

MATERIALS:

- 70cm x 50cm (20in x 28in) mohair fabric with a 2.5cm (1in) pile
- 35mm (1³/₈ in) cotter pin joint set for head
- Set of four 35mm (1¹/₄in) joints for body, locknut or cotter pins
- 9mm (³/₈in) glass eyes
- Black embroidery thread or Perle cotton for nose
- Dental floss
- Matching strong sewing thread
- Polyester filing
- 2 cups plastic pellets
- Fabric-marking pen
- Long doll needle
- Awl
- small sharp scissors
- Ring spanner for fit locknuts
- Small screwdriver
- Small pliers
- Stuffing stick
- Template plastic
- General sewing requirements
- For pinafore: 1m x 35cm (1¹/₈yd x 14in) medium weight striped fabric
- 3 x 1cm (³/₈in) buttons
- Size 2 black patent shoes and size 0 baby socks were used on our bear

firm, as they will loosen up when Georgia is stuffed. Legs are jointed as for the arms.

STUFFING

If you are dressing Georgia, stuff her feet very firmly while they are inside her shoes and socks. This will help her to stand. Stuff her arms and legs before stuffing her body, making sure to use only small amounts of stuffing at a time. Mould each piece as you go. Georgia stands by herself so fill her legs firmly. When satisfied with stuffing, sew up seams with Ladder Stitch using dental floss. Make sure no stitches are visible and finish securely.

Body: Place a small amount of stuffing in the crotch, then fill with plastic pellets. Push filling down with stuffing stick, making sure shoulders and neck are filled firmly and evenly. Sew back seam with Ladder Stitch.

Eyes: Mark desired location of eyes on Georgia's head and make holes with the awl. Insert a long piece of doubled dental floss through the wire loop on the eye, then thread all four threads through a large doll needle. Push the needle through the hole. Bring it out at the back of he head at the neck. Repeat with other eye, bringing needle out close to first threads. Pull the threads and tie off using a reef knot. Make sure the eye are very firmly secured.

Nose: The nose shape you desire can be drawn on your bear's face with an erasable pen. Stitch the nose with doubled black embroidery cotton in Satin Stitch, keeping stitches even, firm and close together. Repeat, filling in any gaps.

Mouth: Bring the thread through to the bottom centre of nose. Stitch the mouth in an inverted Y. Trim back excess mohair if needed. Make sure all seams are brushed and gently tease out any fur caught in the stitching.

PINAFORE

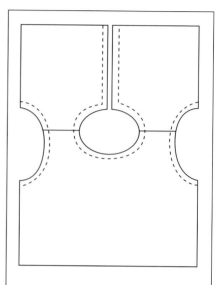

Place bodice and lining together and stitch centre backs, neckline and armholes. Turn backs out through the shoulders.

Trace the pattern, transferring all markings and cut out. If the fabric is striped, the stripes should run vertically on the finished pinafore. A 1cm seam allowance is included in the pattern.

Bodice: With right sides facing, stitch the front and back bodice together at the shoulder seam and repeat for the lining. Place the bodice and lining right sides together and stitch up the centre back, around the neckline and down the other side of centre back. stitch around armholes. Turn right side out by gently easing the backs through the shoulders. Stitch the bodice and lining side seams in one line.

Skirt: Zigzag or overlock around all edges of the skirt piece. Mark and fold pleats approximately 2cm apart and 1.5cm deep. If you are using striped fabric, use the stripes to gauge the size of your pleats. Stitch around the top of the skirt, securing the pleats. Adjust skirt to fit the bodice, leaving 2cm of fabric extending on each side at the centre back. Stitch skirt to bodice with right sides together. Turn

under the overlocked edge of the centre back skirt in line with bodice, then press. Pin bodice and skirt backs together, matching the centre back marks, then stitch the skirt centre back seam in the fold of the top layer of fabric. Leave 4cm open at the top of the skirt to form a placket.

Make three buttonholes on the back bodice or attach press-studs sew buttons over. Cut a strip of fabric to fit around your bear's head, fray the edges and tie in a big bow. ❉

Boo Bear

*Boo Bear delights in making mischief. Designed by
Lynette Le-Roy of Thread Bearz Academy of Craft, this modern
bear has flexible fingers and is stuffed with pellets and
fire-retardant wood wool.*

PREPARATION

Stroke the fur fabric to find the direction of the pile. Trace pattern pieces onto paper and transfer onto the wrong side of the fur fabric, reversing pieces where indicated and transferring all markings. Cut out carefully. Cut the muzzle, inner ears, tummy and foot pads from the felt. A 5mm (¼in) seam allowance is been included on the pattern pieces.

Note: If this bear to be given to a baby or small child, we recommend you do not use glass or plastic pellets to fill the bear.

MAKING THE HEAD

With right sides together, join side head pieces to the head gusset pieces. Double-stitch all seams. Join the two muzzle pieces together at the centre and insert and join the chin gusset. With the right sides together, join the muzzle onto the side faces, centring the nose seam and leaving the neck open. turn right side out and stuff the head firmly.

Eyes: In desired eye positions, make a hole large enough to accommodate the shank at the back of the eye. With a double strand of dental floss, make a loop through the eye shank and thread into a long doll needle. Pass the threaded needle through the eye hole and exit at the base of the neck. Repeat for the other eye. To sink the eyes into the head, pull threads firmly. Tie the ends together firmly to finish off. If you wish to have felt on the back of he eyes, coat the back of the felt with craft glue and slip into position over the eyes.

Nose and Mouth: Trace and cut template of the nose. Trace around it on the bear's muzzle. Using the black DMC embroidery thread, fill in the nose with even, close–together satin stitches. If you want a raised nose, simply stitch over the template a number of times. Stitch the mouth in a Running Stitch.

Ears: With the right sides together, stitch ears along the curved edge, leaving the bottom straight edge open. Top-stitch the inner ears to inside ear pieces. Using strong thread, sew bottom edge of ears together with Ladder Stitch. Stitch ears to head in the appropriate position, sewing twice for added strength.

Body: With right sides facing, join the two back pieces together, leaving the opening in the centre back. With right sides facing, ease both tummy inserts to fit the side body pieces. When both halves are set in position, stitch together at the front tummy centre seam from the neck down to the bottom. Join the front body to the back body.

Legs: With the right sides together, stitch legs leaving an opening at the back. pin the sole onto foot with right sides facing and tack into position. Sew and turn right side out.

Arms: With right sides together, stitch arms leaving opening at the back. Turn right side out and topstitch two rows of stitching on hands to create three fingers and one thumb. To give your bear flexible fingers insert chenille sticks into finger and thumb channels. Using the stuffing tool pack rest of hands with small amounts of fill. Stuff remainder of arms after jointing.

JOINTING

Using the awl, make a hole in the limbs and body at the joint marks. Take a cotter pin, place a washer onto it and then a wooden disc. Place this joint section inside the bear's leg or arm, making sure the cotter pin protrudes out through the joint hole. Now push the protruding

FINISHED SIZE

• 33cm (13in)

MATERIALS

• 1m x 25cm (⅛yd x 10in) Short pile mohair
• 6 x 3.8cm (1½in) discs, matching washers and cotter pins for arm joints.
• Chenille sticks for wiring hands
• Square of mottled felt for tummy, muzzle and eyes.
• 12mm (½in) glass eyes
• No. 5 DMC or black cotton thread for nose
• 250grm (9oz) wood wool stuffing
• Plastic pellets for tummy (see note)
• Dental floss or strong thread
• Long doll needle
• Stuffing tool
• Awl
• Long-nosed pliers
• Craft glue for backs of eyes (optional)
• Tracing paper
• General sewing requirements

off. Place matching disc and washer in the neck of the body and sew a running stich around neck. Gather, leaving a small hole for the cotter pin. Push cotter pin protruding from the head into the body and thread through disc and washer. Curl over shanks of split pin with pliers to secure.

Tail: With the right sides together, stitch two halves and turn out through the tail bottom. Stuff with a small amount of stuffing. Stitch onto bear with a Ladder Stitch.

cotter pin through he corresponding joint position in the body. On the inside body, place a wooden disc and a washer over the cotter pin. Using the pliers, curl over the cotter pin shanks to secure joints firmly in place.

Head: Thread a cotter pin with a disc and a washer, then place inside head. Using a strong thread, do running-stitch around the base of the neck, pulling tightly to make the disc fit snugly and end

STUFFING

Using the stuffing stick, firmly stuff all limbs and ladder-stitch the opening close. Stuff around the neck and shoulders with stuffing and fill his belly with pellets. Close the opening with Ladder Stitch. ❊

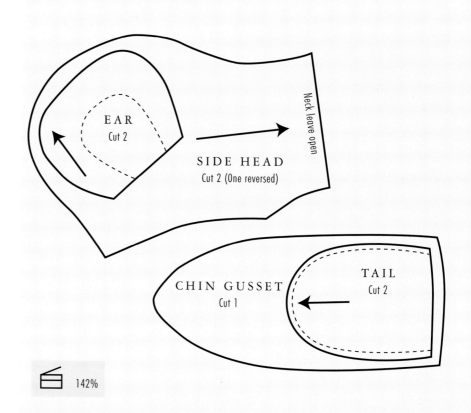

142%

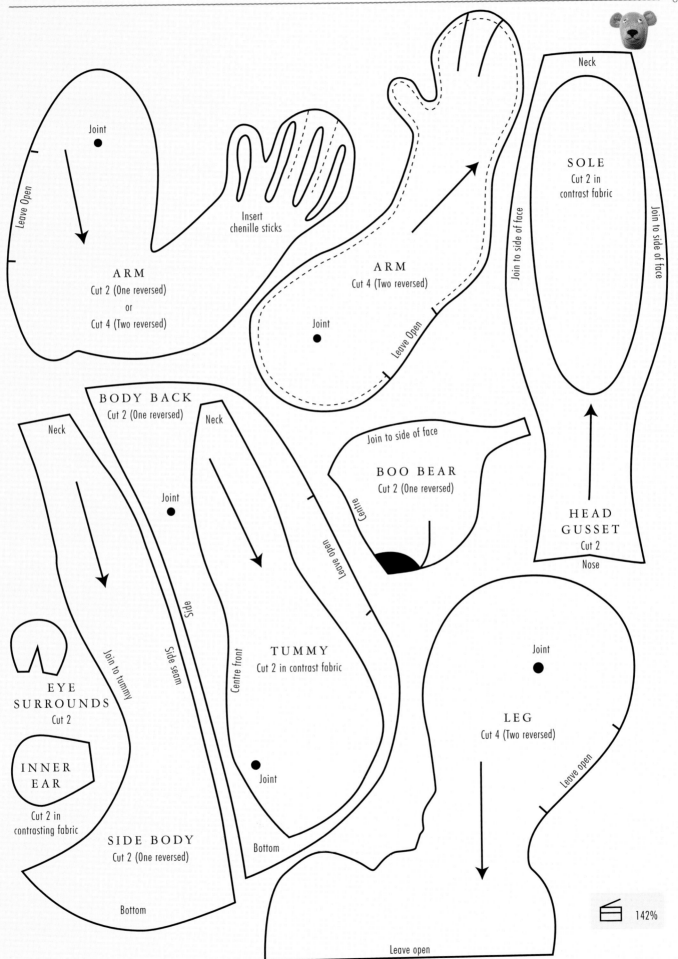

Joint

Leave Open

ARM
Cut 2 (One reversed)
or
Cut 4 (Two reversed)

Insert
chenille sticks

ARM
Cut 4 (Two reversed)

Joint

Leave Open

Neck

SOLE
Cut 2 in
contrast fabric

Join to side of face

Join to side of face

BODY BACK
Cut 2 (One reversed)

Neck

Neck

Joint

Join to side of face

Join to tummy

Side

Side seam

Centre front

Centre

Leave open

BOO BEAR
Cut 2 (One reversed)

**HEAD
GUSSET**
Cut 2

Nose

**EYE
SURROUNDS**
Cut 2

**INNER
EAR**
Cut 2 in
contrasting fabric

TUMMY
Cut 2 in contrast fabric

Joint

Joint

Joint

Joint

LEG
Cut 4 (Two reversed)

Leave open

Bottom

SIDE BODY
Cut 2 (One reversed)

Bottom

Bottom

Leave open

142%

Dorothy

Dorothy is well protected from the colder days ahead with her longer coat and pretty shawl. Monica Spicer has designed this quaint little bear who's full of character, to add to your collection.

PREPARATION

Read instructions carefully before you begin. Trace the pattern onto tracing paper, transferring all markings and glue onto cardboard. Place pattern pieces onto the back of the fabric so the arrows follow the direction of the fur pile. Cut out using the tip of the scissors, cutting only the backing fabric and not the pile. A 3mm seam allowance is included in the pattern

HEAD

Sew the head pieces together from the nose to the front of the neck edge. Join the head gusset from the nose to the back of the neck edge on one side, then repeat for the other side. Turn right side out and stuff the head firmly. Run a gathering thread around the neck edge, using upholstery thread. Place a T-pin through a disc and place them inside the neck, with the pin protruding. Draw in the gathering thread tight around the pin and tie off with a couple of knots.

EARS

With right sides together, stitch around the curved edge, leaving the base open. Turn right side out and baste the open edges together. Position on the head with a couple of pins and sew firmly in place using Ladder Stitch.

NOSE

Ensure the fur on the muzzle is clipped very short, cutting just a little fur at a time. Trim back to the eyes and around the jaw. Glue the nose template in place and embroider the nose with the Perlé cotton using Satin Stitch. Form the mouth with straight stitches.

EYES

Make two small holes in the head with the awl for the eye placement. Insert a long piece of upholstery thread through the wire loop of the eye. Thread the two ends onto a long needle and insert through the eye hole, take the needle through the head and bring it out behind the opposite ear. Finish with a couple of knots. Repeat for the other eye.

BODY

Sew the body pieces together, leaving an opening at the back for stuffing and at he neck for the joint. Make a hole at the joint marks using an awl. Turn right side out. Place the T-pin protruding from the head into the neck of the body and attach a disc. Separate the ends of the pin and turn each end over onto the disc using the long-nose pliers so the head is held firmly.

ARMS AND LEGS

Sew the paw pads to the inner arms, then sew the inner and outer arms together with right sides facing, leaving an

FINISHED SIZE

• 18cm (7in)

MATERIALS

• 30cm x 25cm (12in x 10in) mohair
• Small piece leather for paw pads
• 5mm ($\frac{1}{4}$in) black glass eyes
• 10 x 20mm ($\frac{3}{4}$in) fibreboard discs
• 5 x 13 mm ($\frac{1}{2}$in) mini T-pins
• No 8 black Perle cotton
• Small piece of felt for nose
• Matching sewing thread
• Upholstery thread
• Polyester stuffing
• Glass beads
• Craft glue
• Small pointed scissors
• Stuffing tool
• Long-nose pliers
• Felt-tip pen
• Awl
• Tweezers
• General sewing requirements

opening where indicated. Make a hole on the inner arm at the joint mark and turn right side out. Sew around the legs leaving an opening at the back and leaving the base of the foot open. Match the centre back and front of the foot pads to the leg seams and stitch in place. Make a hole on the inner leg at the joint position and turn right side out,

around the joints with polyester stuffing. Fill the middle of the body with glass beads, then close the opening with Ladder Stitch. Attach the limbs to the body in the same manner as for the head, then stuff the base of the body and around the joints with polyester stuffing. Fill the middle of the body with glass beads, then close the opening with Ladder Stitch.

JOINTING LIMBS TO BODY

Make up the limb joints as for the head and place inside the limb. Stuff the limbs firmly and close the openings with Ladder Stitch. Attach the limbs to the body in the same manner as for the head, then stuff the base of the body and

FINISHING

Pick out the fur pile trapped in the seams using tweezers and give Dorothy a good brush. Make her look pretty with a couple of flowers in her hair and perhaps give her a pretty knitted or lace shawl fastened with an attractive brooch.❁

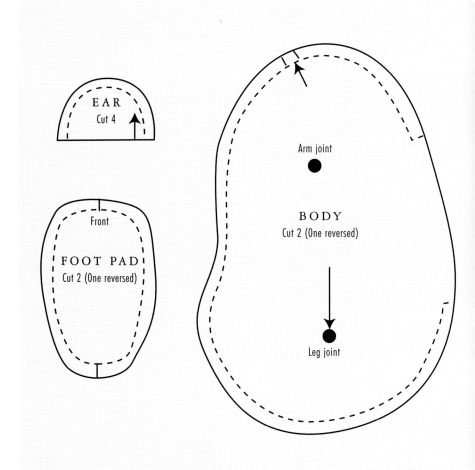

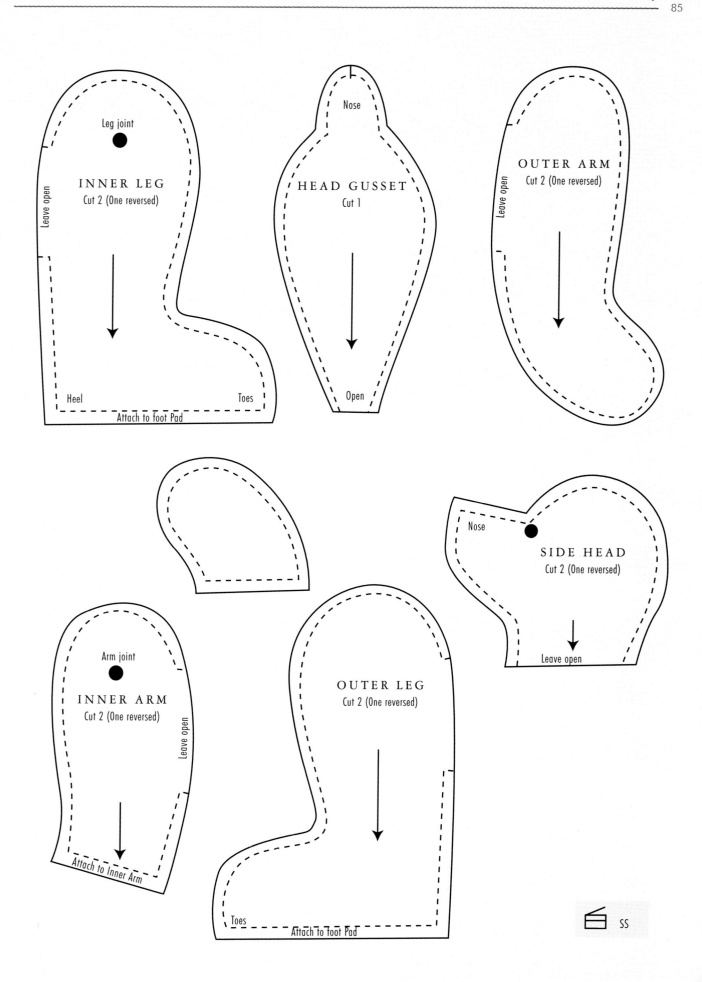

Madame Martine
with her Aubergine

Dawn Nicholl has created another of her whimsical bears to add to your collection. With her expressive face and eyes, botanical print apron and Aubergine, Madame Martine will be sure to attract many admiring comments.

PREPARATION

Trace the pattern pieces from the pattern sheet and transfer all the relevant markings. Following the layout diagram place the pattern pieces on the wrong side of the fur, reversing the pieces where indicated. Trace around each piece with the felt tip pen. Before commencing to cut the fabric, check that the pieces have been reversed correctly to make up the relevant pairs.

Using the small sharp scissors, cut out the pattern pieces taking care to cut the backing only and avoid cutting through the fur pile. From the calico cut two pieces for Madame Martine's body.

SEWING AND STUFFING THE PIECES

With right sides together, tack and then stitch around the pieces. Stitch around the head leaving open at the base for attaching to the body. Sew around the arms and legs leaving open at the top for stuffing. Stitch the curved edges of the ears together. To form the muzzle, stitch from the nose point to the base (B) on the muzzle sides, then stitch the curved edges of the muzzle top to the muzzle sides. Stuff the head and shoulders, noting that the face is kept relatively flat but firm. Take special care when stuffing the neck area as this should be well stuffed to avoid the head wobbling. Stuff the legs and arms firmly up to the stitching line. Stitch across this line to hold the stuffing in place, leaving the top 5cm (2in) of the arms and legs unstuffed.

MAKING THE BODY

Sew around the calico body pieces stitching in the legs at the base where indicated on the pattern. Ensure the legs will swing free when the body is turned to the right side. Following the directions on the pattern piece, leaving an opening at the top for stuffing. Turn to right side and stuff the body firmly. Ladder-stitch the stuffed body to the base of the head and shoulders adding more stuffing as you go to ensure the seam join and shoulder areas are as filmy packed as the rest of the bear. Turn in the raw edges at the top of the arms and to attach to the body where indicated on the pattern making sure that the arms are facing forward.

FORMING THE FACE

Ladder-stitch the muzzle to the point indicated of the pattern adding more stuffing as you stitch in the same manner as for the shoulder. Turn in the raw edges of the ears and stitch to the head where shown on the pattern. Fray the edges of the eyelids by cutting 1cm (^{3}/$_8$in) slits as shown on the pattern. Cut a hole in the

FINISHED SIZE

• 63cm (25in)

MATERIALS:

• 75cm x 50cm (30in x 20in) sparse mohair (short and spiky). The fur used for our Madame Martine has no nap, if your fur has a definite nap please allow for the extra quantity needed.

• 35cm x 25cm (14in x 10in) piece of calico

• Two 10mm (^{3}/$_8$in) black shank buttons for eyes

• Black Perlé cotton for nose and mouth

• Extra strong thread

• Sewing thread to match mohair

• Polyester stuffing

• Felt tip pen

• Small sharp scissors

• Extra long doll needle

MADAME MARTINE'S CLOTHES

(Apron, Dress, Hat and Knickers)

- 50cm x 115cm (20in x 45in) of a botanical print fabric
- 1m x 115cm (40in x 45in) calico
- 1 x 5g skein of Perlé cotton in a colour to complement the print
- Sewing thread to match print fabric and calico
- One button for apron
- Two press studs
- 31cm (12in) of narrow elastic
- Darning needle

eyelid through which to insert the shank of the button eye. Push the shank of the button through the hole from the wrong side of the fur fabric. Thread a piece of strong thread through the shank and then thread the two ends through your doll needle. Insert the needle through the eye position, bringing the needle out at the back of the head. Repeat for the other eye. Tie the four threads together and lose the ends back inside the head. Using the black Perlé thread, embroider the nose and smiling mouth, following the illustration on pattern sheet.

Note: To place and cut out the pattern pieces for the clothes as per the layout diagrams, the hat edge and centre, sleeve, front bodice and knickers will need to be traced out in mirror image down the edge marked 'pattern fold'. There are no actual pattern pieces for the apron skirt or the dress skirt appearing on the pattern sheet, however measurements for these are given on the sheet.

DRESS

Stitch both front and back neck flounces together matching the * at the shoulder seams. Place the two flounce pieces together, with right sides facing. Stitch around the two ends and outside curve. Clip the seams, turn and press.

With right sides facing, stitch the bodice front and backs together at the shoulder seams, neaten and press open. Turn in a narrow hem along the raw edge of the bodice back, press, turn in again and stitch. Fold to the inside along the facing fold line and press. Stitch the flounce to the neck edge by placing the WRONG side of the bodice to the RIGHT side of the flounce, matching the ends of the flounce with the back bodice

facing edge. Clip the seam and turn the flounce to the right side, press. Thread a darning needle with a length of Perlé thread, knot one end. At the centre back make a single stitch through the bodice and flounce 1cm (³/₈in) down from the neck edge. Then, leaving 25cm (10in) of thread hanging free to tie into a bow, secure the thread with a French Knot. Using a simple Running Stitch, stitch around the neck edge, secure with a French Knot at the opposite centre back and leave a similar length to tie into a bow.

Gather sleeves where marked on pattern, pull up gathers to fit bodice armholes. With right sides together, stitch sleeves to the bodice, neaten seams. Stitch in one line from the sleeve hem through to the bodice edge. Neaten. Turn raw edge of sleeve in twice and stitch.

Turn in and stitch the centre back edges of the skirt to correspond with the centre back seams of the bodice. Gather the waist edge of the skirt to fit the bodice edge. With right sides together stitch into place, neaten seam.

Stitch the centre back seam of the dress from the hem edge up to 8cm (3in) from the waist edge. Press open. Turn up a hem on the skirt and stitch. Place the dress on Madame Martine and, taking care not to stitch into her arms, stitch a row of smocking gathers around the sleeve 3cm (1¹/₄in) up from the hem to form the frill. Attach two press studs to the bodice back where indicated on the pattern.

APRON

Turn in a narrow hem on the raw edge of the apron centre back edges and the hemline, turn in again and stitch. Hem the curved edges of the frills and gather along the straight edge. Pull up to fit between the *marked on the shoulder strap. Sandwich the frills between two shoulder straps with right sides facing, stitch then turn to right side and press. Repeat for other strap.

Turn in a narrow hem on the raw edges of the shoulder straps and press. Fold apron bib in half along the fold line, wrong sides together. With the fold line forming the top of the bib, sandwich the bib between the shoulder straps and stitch the edges together. Gather the apron skirt to fit between the * marked on the waistband, stitch to front waistband. Stitch the bib to the other edge of the waistband matching the centre fronts Pin the other ends of the straps to the waistband where indicated on the pattern. With right sides facing, place the waistbands together as for a facing. Stitch the ends of the band and across the top ensuring that you have stitched in the straps and bib. Trim seam, turn in the raw edge and handstitch to the skirt edge. Make a buttonhole and attach button to correspond.

HAT

❖

With right sides together, sew two close rows of stitching around the outer edges of the hat brim, clip close to the stitching, turn to right side and press. Press small turnings inwards on the raw edges of the brims. Sandwich the print centre between the hat brims. Pin, tack and stitch making sure to stitch through all layers. With your needle threaded with Perlé cotton, run a gathering stitch around the edges where the print meets the calico. Pull up to fit Madame Martine's head, tie in a bow and place on her head.

KNICKERS

With right sides together, stitch from the crotch to the waist edge on both the front and back seams, neaten edges. To form legs, stitch from one hem edge up to crotch then down to the other hem edge, neaten. Turn in raw edge at waist edge, turn in again and stitch, thus forming a casing for the elastic. Turn up hems on the leg edges then stitch a row of smocking gathers in the same manner as for the sleeves. Thread elastic through waist casing.

Aubergine

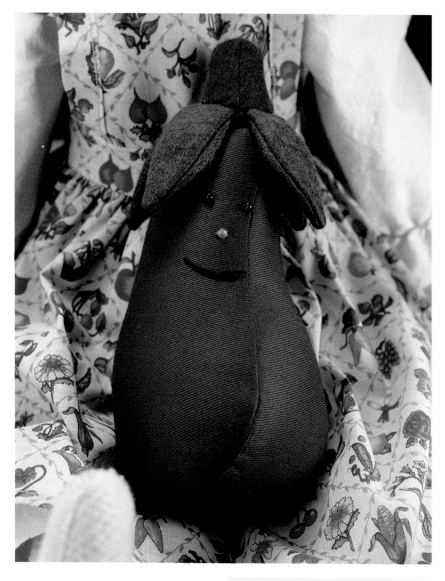

To prepare the gusset pattern piece, match the line marked A to B. Lay this and the side pieces onto the purple fabric and cut out. Cut out the leaves from the bright green felt and the stalk from the dark green felt.

MAKING THE AUBERGINE

Starting at the top and with right sides together, stitch the side pieces to the gusset matching the dots all the way around. Make slash where marked on pattern and turn to right side through the slash. Stuff, then close the slash. Stitch around, make slash where indicated and turn to right side. Stitch the slash closed. Stitch the stalk seams together to form a thimble shape, turn and stuff. Slip-stitch stalk to upper side of leaves, turning in the edges as you stitch. Glue the leaves and stalk to top of aubergine with craft glue, placing the glue in a cross shape part way down the leaves.

Form the face by attaching the beads and stitching the mouth as shown on the patten.

Now Madam Martine is ready to join her friends in the vegetable garden. ✿

THE AUBERGINE
MATERIALS

- 16cm x 46cm (6¹/₂in x 18in) purple fabric for aubergine
- 14cm x 25cm (5³/₄in x 10in) bright green felt for leaves
- 10cm x 10cm (4in x 4in) dark green felt for stalk
- Sewing thread to match
- Black embroidery thread
- One pink and two black beads
- Craft Glue

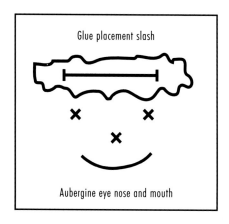

Glue placement slash

Aubergine eye nose and mouth

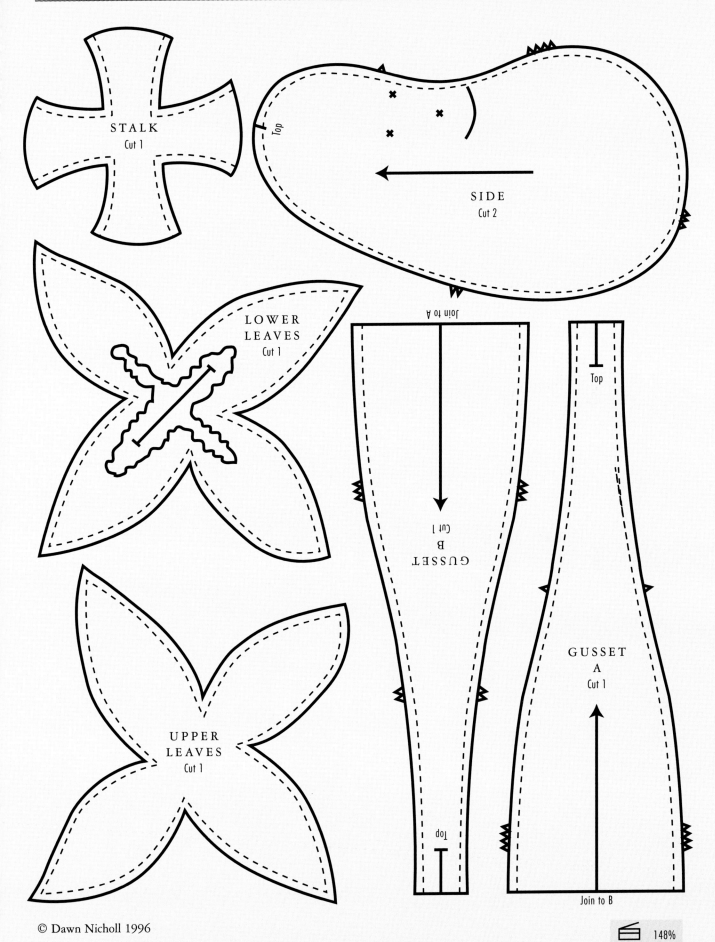

STALK
Cut 1

Top

SIDE
Cut 2

LOWER
LEAVES
Cut 1

Join to A

GUSSET
B
Cut 1

Top

GUSSET
A
Cut 1

UPPER
LEAVES
Cut 1

Top

Top

Join to B

© Dawn Nicholl 1996

148%

Bear Basics

*These guidelines offer basic advice to those new to the pleasures
of bear making. However, each project also has its own set of instructions
and these may vary from the guidelines below as every bear maker
has his or her own personal style. Bear making is much easier with
the right equipment and it is a good idea to assemble a kit containing all
your basic tools before you start. A plastic tool box is ideal for keeping your
tools together and for storing your current, unfinished project.*

BASIC TOOL KIT

- Tracing paper
- Lightweight cardboard or quilter's plastic
- Glue stick
- Fine felt-tip pens
- Scissors to cut paper and cardboard
- Small, sharp scissors to cut fur fabric
- Sewing threads to match fur
- Sewing needles
- New needle for sewing machine (if machine sewing your bear)
- Thimble
- Tweezers
- Stuffing tool (wooden or metal)
- Long-nose pliers
- Screwdriver and ratchet spanner (for joints with nuts and bolts)
- Coloured-head pins
- Strong thread or dental floss for closing stuffing holes
- Long doll needles
- Embroidery needles
- Embroidery thread for nose
- Brush for fur
- Selection of ribbons for a perfect finishing touch

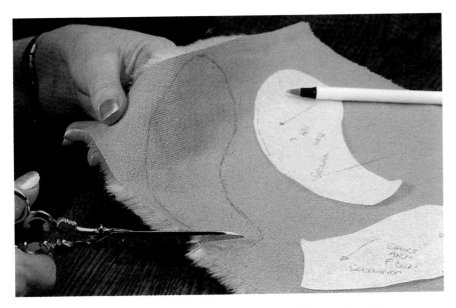

Before you machine-stitch, tack the pieces together using overcast stitch, tucking the fur in with the needle as you go.

Use small, sharp scissors to cut out the pieces, being careful to cut only through the backing fabric and not through the fur itself.

Gathering your tools

❖

It pays to assemble a basic kit of bear-making equipment before you begin to make a bear.

As well as your chosen pattern and fabric, you will need a pair of small, sharp scissors, a doll needle for button, bead or wire-backed glass eyes, a fine felt-tip pen and joints of a suitable size.

Use safety eyes if you are making bears for children under the age of three.

Commercially packed joint sets are the easiest option – but you can make up sets yourself by purchasing the right sizes of wooden discs, metal washers and split pins or nuts and bolts. Leather washers can be useful next to the fabric for extra wear.

You will also need a small pair of long-nose pliers, some extra-strong thread, for gathering or inserting the eyes, embroidery thread or Perlé cotton for the nose and thread to match the fur fabric you are using.

You can save time and achieve a better result by using a stuffing stick.

Cutting out the pattern

❖

If you think you will be making several bears with the same pattern, glue the pattern sheet onto some lightweight card before you cut it out. Mark the reference points – joint pin marks, notch marks and pile direction arrows – on both sides of the pattern pieces so that they are easier to transfer to your fabric. It's a good idea to mark one side in another colour so that you can clearly see when you are reversing the pieces to make pairs.

Once you have prepared your pattern, arrange the pieces on the reverse side of your fur fabric and trace around each piece with a felt-tip pen. Trace all pieces onto the fabric and check them before you begin cutting out.

When you cut fur fabric, try not to cut the pile itself. It is easier to use small scissors and slide the lower blade through the fur pile so that only the backing is cut. If you are happy to use a craft knife instead, have a practice run on the fabric before starting on the marked pieces.

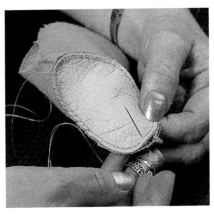

Before hand-sewing, overcast the edges of all fabric with woven backing. Use a close, even backstitch to sew the seams.

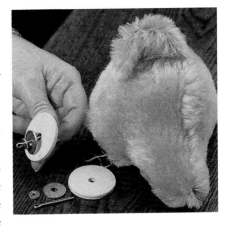

To assemble a split-pin joint, slip a metal washer and then a wooden disc onto the split pin. If there is a danger of the metal washer slipping over the head of the pin, insert a smaller washer first.

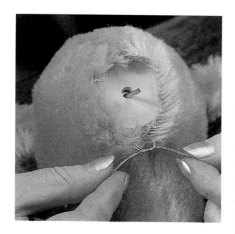

After inserting the joint into the head, run a line of gathering around the base of the head and gently pull up both ends of the thread until the fabric fits tightly around the protruding pin. Secure with a triple knot.

Insert the pin from the head through the neck of the body, slip on the wooden disc and then the washer. Use the long-nose pliers to turn the ends of the pin over.

Use a stuffing stick to push the stuffing right to the ends of the limbs.

Sewing Teddy

If you are sewing by machine, you will be happier with the final result if you first tack the pieces together by hand using a wide overcast stitch and stroking the fur into the seam with your needle as you go. It is well worth doing this just to minimise the time you would otherwise spend gently hooking the fur out of each seam after the bear is finished. If your fabric has a woven backing, use this technique before hand sewing as well. A close, even backstitch will give the best results if you are sewing a woven backing by hand, while a close overcast stitch is ideal for knit-back fabrics. Always use a double thread for hand sewing and draw it up firmly to create solid seams.

Jointing a bear

There are many ways to attach the limbs and head of a bear to its body. Miniature bears are perfectly happy with their arms and legs threaded through with strong thread. Buttons can be added to reinforce the joints on larger bears jointed in this way. External joints like these are popular because they don't need special equipment and are easy to do.

Internal joints allow the bear's arms and legs to move which gives a more lifelike appearance and allows the limbs to be 'posed' in various ways.

A standard traditional bear requires five sets of joints – one for the head and one for each arm and leg.

Many bear makers prefer to use the 'traditional' wooden joints and split pins. However, you can also purchase wooden joints with nuts and bolts instead of split pins, or even moulded plastic joint systems are available.

When assembling wooden joints, put a metal washer over the split pin first, followed by a wooden disc. It is important to ensure that the head of each split pin cannot be pulled through the metal washers. If you suspect that you may be able to pull one through, place a washer with a smaller hole onto the pin first.

Stuffing the head

When you have sewn up all the parts of your bear, turn them the right way out. If you are using safety eyes they are inserted before you stuff the head; other eyes are inserted after stuffing. Check that the reference points for the eyes are an equal distance from the centre of the nose before you insert the safety eyes.

When stuffing the head, begin with small pieces in the nose so that you make it firm enough to embroider, and then fill the rest of the head. Your neck joint (one of the larger ones if your joint set has two sizes) sits inside the neck on top of the stuffing with the pin sticking out. With the extra-strong thread run a gathering stitch around the edge of the neck, leaving a 'tail' of thread at both ends. By drawing up both ends of the gathering thread tightly, the fabric will close around the pin and you can then tie the ends together with a triple knot.

Attaching the head to the body

Depending on the pattern, the neck of the body may also have to be closed with a gathering thread. Use the same method as you did for gathering the base of the head, remembering to leave a small gap

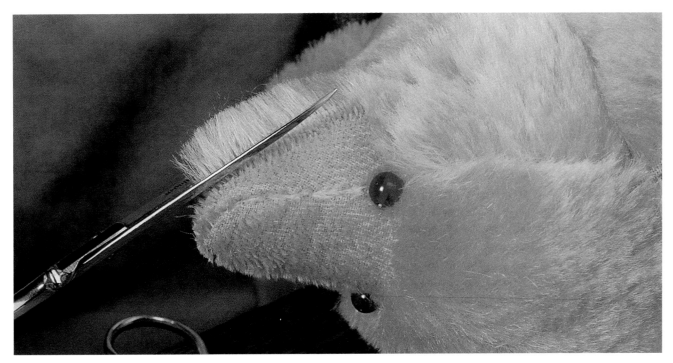

Trim fur from the muzzle before you embroider the nose. How much of the muzzle you 'shave' is up to you and the effect you wish to achieve.

for the head pin to go through. Push the head pin through the top of the body and slip one of the large-size wooden discs and then a washer onto it inside the body. Using long-nosed pliers, turn the ends of the pins over so they hold both the neck discs together tightly. If using a nut and bolt joint system, slip the bolt protruding from the head into the gap at the top of the body and place a metal washer, then a nut over the bolt inside the body. Tighten with a spanner.

Stuffing the limbs

❖

Beginning with small amounts, stuff the bear's feet. Compare the shapes of the footpads to see if you have definite left and right feet before inserting the larger size joints. The joint pins should be pushed gently through the fabric of the inner side of each leg at the joint pin mark. By holding the pin firmly on the outside you can fill the rest of the leg without getting any stuffing between the inner leg fabric and the joint disc.

Use the extra-strong thread to close the openings with ladder stitch – this stitch is worked from the right side of the fabric.

The arms are finished in exactly the same way as the legs, using the smaller size joints with the pin protruding through the fabric on the paw side. It is easier to finish all four pieces before attaching them to the body.

Assembling the bear

❖

Once your arms and legs are complete, find the joint marks inside the body. Push the pin from one arm through the body fabric at the upper joint mark. Hold the pin and double check that you have the right arm on the right side. Then place one of the smaller wooden discs and washers onto the pin inside the body and turn each end of the split pin over as you did for the neck. Check that the joint is firm and tighten if necessary. The same procedure should be followed for the other arm and both legs.

 ENLARGING
THE PATTERNS
Most patterns in this book need to be enlarged before use. To do this accurately, look for the photocopy symbol and number on the pattern (for example ⊟30%), set the photocopier to the percentage given and photocopy each piece on this setting.

Embroider the nose using an even satin stitch.

Giving Teddy a face

❖

Now that your bear is together, you can give him or her a unique personality. Take your time with the features as the size, shape and placement of ears, eyes and nose all have a bearing on character.

EYES

If you are not using safety eyes, mark the eye positions with glass-headed pins, and double thread the doll needle with extra-strong thread. Direct the needle from the centre back of the bear's neck, just above the joint disc, through the head to the position of the right eye, leaving a tail of thread hanging at the back of the neck. Thread on the first eye and then take the needle through the top of the muzzle to the position of the left eye. Thread the second eye on and then take the needle back through the head to the

point where you began. Draw both ends of the thread up firmly and evenly to set the eyes in the head and give the bear more expression. Triple knot the ends of the thread and lose the ends directing the needle into the head just beside the knot, out under the ear and clipping the thread off there.

EARS

Many patterns require the ears to be attached when the head is finished. The easiest way to do this is to pin the ears directly to the head and ladder-stitch around both edges. Some bear artists like to sew the bottom edges of the ear together before they stitch them on – this is just a matter of personal preference.

SHAVING THE MUZZLE

Many of the traditional mohair bears have 'shaved' muzzles. This is achieved by

laying the scissor blades flat against the 'skin' and clipping the fur around the muzzle to the desired length.

Face trimming can be a daunting task for a beginner, but if you take only a little off the length of the pile at a time, you should have no major problems.

Before you begin embroidering the nose, the fur at the tip of the nose should be trimmed right down to the backing fabric. How much more of the bear's muzzle you trim depends on the look you want to achieve and your expertise.

If you want to trim only the area under the nose, take a little at a time so that there will be no bald patches around your embroidery.

If you decide to trim no further than the nose itself, at least make sure the eyes are visible by taking excess fur from just inside and below each eye.

EMBROIDERING THE NOSE

The size and shape of your bear's nose and mouth are entirely up to you. To achieve a nice, even shape it is best to begin by stitching an outline for the nose and then filling in with satin stitch. The most important thing to remember with nose embroidery is to keep your stitch tension even.

Noses can be built up in several layers and can be done in different colours – the variety is what makes every bear a unique individual.

Finishing

❖

Now that your bear has acquired a distinct character and all the limbs are attached, all that is needed to make your bear come fully to life is to stuff the body and to close the opening with ladder stitch.

A neck ribbon, scarf or a pretty dress or jacket will give your bear the final, individual touch.

Bear Stitches

The patterns in this book give guidance on which stitches to use for each step of the bear-making process. For those unfamiliar with these stitches, we have provided the following stitch guide.

Overcast (TOP stitch or Whipstitch)

If machine stitching, it pays to first hand-tack your pieces together with a wide overcast stitch. This not only prevents the fur pieces slipping while machining, but also helps to keep long fur away from the seams where it can become tangled. When hand sewing fabrics with a woven backing, a much better result will be achieved by joining the pieces with a wide overcast stitch before you backstitch the fabric. Refer to photograph on page 15.

Backstitch

Use a close, even backstitch to hand sew seams. Always use a double thickness of thread and pull the thread firmly so that stitches will not show through the seam.

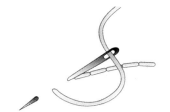

Backstitch

Stab stitch

This stitch is similar to backstitch but is more suitable for some fabrics, especially thick ones, as the needle is pushed through from one side of the fabric to the other and the thread pulled tight before taking the needle back to the first side. It takes a little longer than backstitch, but the stitches can be made smaller and tighter.

Ladder stitch

This stitch is used to close openings left for stuffing and turning. It is worked on the right side of the fabric with strong thread. Stitch along the seam allowance line and pull the thread tight at each stitch to close the opening.

Satin Stitch

Teddy-bear noses are normally sewn in satin stitch. For the best effect, take the needle in and out as close as you can to the last stitch. You can outline the nose shape in backstitch as a guide. Satin-stitch over the backstitch outline to cover it up.

Gathering (or Running) Stitch

The fabric at the base of the head is gathered around the neck joint. In some patterns, the neck edge of the body is also gathered. Take small, even stitches along the seamline and gently pull both ends of the thread until the fabric closes around the bolt, then tie the two ends together firmly.

Blanket Stitch

This stitch is ideal for neatening raw edges on thick fabrics to prevent them fraying. If sewn with embroidery thread, it can also be used as a decorative edging.

Satin stitch

Stab stitch

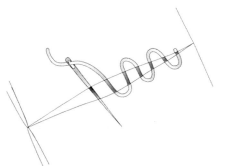

Ladderstitch

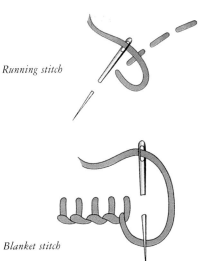

Running stitch

Blanket stitch

Published by
Craftworld Books
A division of Express Publications Pty Ltd, ACN 057 807 904
Under licence from EP Investments Pty Ltd, ACN 003 109 055 (1995)

2 Stanley Street
Silverwater NSW 2128
Australia

First published by Craftworld Books 1999

Publisher Roslyn Smith
Photographic Director Robyn Wilson
Editor Roslyn Smith
Editorial Assistant Melissa Habchi
Designer Annette Tamone

Photographers Tim Connolly, Mark Heriot, Andy Payne
Stylists Abbie Mitchell, Peach Panfili, Charlotte Cruise

National Library of Australia Cataloguing-in-Publication data

Bears to Cherish

ISBN 1875625100

1. Bears

Printed by KHL Printing Co, Singapore

Australian distribution to supermarkets and newsagents by Network Distribution Company, 54 Park Street, Sydney NSW 2000 Ph (02) 9282 8777.

Overseas Distribution Enquiries Godfrey Vella Ph 61 (2) 9748 0599, Locked Bag 111, Silverwater NSW 1811 Australia
email: gvella@expresspublications.com.au